Rich Christians in an Age of Hunger

Rich Christians in an Age of Hunger

A Biblical Study

by

Ronald J. Sider

HODDER AND STOUGHTON
LONDON SYDNEY AUCKLAND TORONTO

All Scripture quotations, unless otherwise indicated, are from the Revised Standard Version of the Bible, copyrighted 1946, 1952, © 1971, 1973.

The diary excerpt quoted on page 24 is from *Beyond All Pity* by Carolina Maria de Jesus, trans. David St. Clair. Copyright © 1962 by Souvenir Press Ltd., and E. P. Dutton & Co. Inc. Reprinted by permission of the publishers.

British Library Cataloguing in Publication Data

Sider, Ronald J
   Rich Christians in an age of hunger.
   1. Christianity and economics
   2. Wealth, Ethics of
   I. Title
   261.8´34´41   BR115.E3

ISBN 0-340-22810-5

Copyright © 1977 by Inter-Varsity Christian Fellowship of the United States of America.

First printed 1978. Second impression 1979.

Printed in Great Britain for
Hodder and Stoughton Limited,
Mill Road, Dunton Green, Sevenoaks, Kent
by Hazell Watson & Viney Ltd, Aylesbury, Bucks

Contents

Acknowledgements

This edition has been completely revised in Parts 1 and 3 and chapter 6 of Part 2 from the original American edition published in 1977. This work was done by a member of the Shaftesbury Project, to whom I am very grateful. I would also like to thank the Revd. Patrick Dearnley, formerly Director of the Shaftesbury Project, members of the Shaftesbury Project overseas aid group, and several people who work in overseas development, for their valuable assistance with this edition. Finally I would like to thank David Watson, Rector of St. Michael-le-Belfrey, York, for writing a foreword to this edition.

The original U.S. edition benefited from the critical comments of many good friends who read parts of the first draft: Judy and John F. Alexander, Arthur Simon, Edgar Stoesz, Richard Taylor, Carol and Merold Westphal. Since I am not an economist, I particularly appreciate the extensive help of two friends who are: Carl Gambs and John Mason. I stubbornly rejected their advice on occasion. Hence they cannot be faulted for the results. But their help and friendship are deeply appreciated.

To Debbie Reumann and Titus Peachy I give special thanks for long hours spent at the typewriter. To Mrs. Anne Allen who typed some of the early chapters, I want to express deep appreciation for her superb secretarial and administrative assistance over several years.

Finally I want to thank *HIS* magazine for publishing an early version of chapter seven, and Ashland Theological Seminary and Emmanuel School of Religion for the opportunity to present parts of this material as public lectures.

Perhaps all books must be lived before they are written.

That is certainly true of books like this one. I must immediately confess that I make no claim to be living out the full implications of this book. But I have begun the pilgrimage. The most important reason I am even a little way down the path is my wife, Arbutus Lichti Sider. Always enthusiastic about a simpler living standard, spontaneously generous and eager to experiment, she has slowly tugged me along. For her critical reading of the manuscript, for our life together without which this book would never have been possible and for her love, I express my deepest appreciation.

The British edition, like the American, is affectionately dedicated to our three children, Theodore Ronald, Michael Jay, and Sonya Maria, who will have to live in the global village we are now creating.

Foreword

IT IS VIRTUALLY impossible to overstress the practical significance of this book. It calls for a new reformation of the church that is as relevant and urgent for today as were Martin Luther's Ninety-Five Theses in 1517.

Certainly there are numerous issues that call for our attention at this present time: confusions over basic doctrines, questions of ordination, patterns of ministry, the role of women, the unity of the church, the place of spiritual gifts, methods of evangelism, the vital need for renewal—these, and many other matters, hammer insistently on the doors of the church.

Nevertheless, while we continue to have an internal, theological dialogue within our own ranks, the harsh, inescapable fact is that *this very day* about 500 million men, women and children throughout the world are literally *starving*, and double that number are undernourished.

The equally disturbing, uncomfortable truth is that Christians in the developed countries are living in comparative gross *affluence*. We have accepted a lifestyle which is so similar to that of the covetous world around us as to be indistinguishable from it. We may try, sometimes with high-sounding spiritual reasons, to justify the money we spend on ourselves, our homes, our food, our clothes, our possessions, our entertainment, our holidays, our children's education, and even our church buildings. We may talk about "trying to win our friends for Christ", about "nothing less than the best being good enough for God", or about "church buildings that must reflect the beauty and glory of our Creator"; yet, however we may describe it, we cannot escape from the fact that (in Jesus' parable of Dives and Lazarus) we are the rich man, clothed and fed in comfort, and also guilty of appalling negligence concerning the starving and sick man at our gate. Since all that we are and all that we possess belong to God, we must one day give account of our stewardship to him.

Further, we have largely ignored the insistent theme throughout the Scriptures—a theme that Ronald Sider expounds so powerfully in this book—that God has always been on the side of the poor. It is not that God is partial towards the poor; he loves equally every person he has created. However, God is essentially a God of justice; and it is because the rich so often oppress or neglect the poor (as is manifestly true in the world of today) that God is especially concerned with the needs of the afflicted. The whole self-revelation of God in the Scriptures—at the time of the Exodus, through the warnings of the prophets, in the compassion of Jesus Christ, with the loving action of the early church—makes this truth abundantly clear.

Moreover, God normally works through his people. If, therefore, we claim to be the people of God, one sure sign of this should be our practical and sacrificial concern for the poor. "If any one has this world's goods and sees his brother in need, yet closes his heart against him, how does God's love abide in him? Little children, let us not love in word or speech but in deed and in truth" (1 John 3:17f). What the apostle John is saying, in his usual forthright terms, is that those who neglect the poor and needy prove that they cannot really be God's children at all, however orthodox and pious their words and beliefs might be.

It is disturbing, therefore, to find that most western Christians are closely identified with the "establishment", with the rich and powerful. We have greater affinity with the affluent and the influential than with the downtrodden and the oppressed. We have accepted a largely middle-class culture, with its worldly values and selfish ambitions, and have conveniently ignored the utterly radical teaching of Jesus concerning money, possessions and social standing within the kingdom of God.

Most serious of all, perhaps, our lifestyle, both individual and corporate, is astonishingly different from the lifestyle of our Master whom we profess to follow and serve. We know (and preach) all about the grace of our Lord Jesus Christ who, though he was rich, for our sakes became poor, really and extremely poor; but we do not demonstrate the same grace in our own lives. We have not become poor so that others might become rich. We have not even chosen to live simply so that others might simply live. We glory in gospel texts, such as John 3:16, which describes God's amazing generosity towards *us* in giving *us* his own Son; but we easily forget certain other texts, such as 1 John 3:16, which challenge our generosity towards *others*: "We ought to lay down our lives for the brethren".

Ronald Sider rightly believes that a new reformation is urgently called for at three levels at the same time.

First, "simple personal lifestyles are crucial to symbolize, validate and facilitate our concern for the hungry". If we carefully and honestly re-examine our own values, and ask ourselves how far these genuinely reflect biblical standards and how far they are controlled by western culture and social convention, most of us could and should live far, far more simply than we do. The biblical principle is that of *equality* amongst God's people (2 Cor. 8:14); and the biblical standard for each Christian is *enough* (2 Cor. 9:8). Everything above "enough" is to "provide . . . for every good work". The example of John Wesley (p. 150) is one probable reason why God was able to use him so powerfully to revive a decadent church and nation.

Second, "the church must change so that its common life presents a new model for a divided world". As I know a little from my own experience, a deliberate attempt to make a radical change in one's own personal and family lifestyle can be so painful and threatening that the need to "immerse ourselves deeply in Christian fellowship", and to "find our primary identity with other brothers and sisters who are also unconditionally committed to biblical values" (p. 164) becomes of considerable importance. Such Christian fellowship, as found in the New Testament means "unconditional availability to and unlimited liability for the other sisters and brothers—emotionally, financially and spiritually". This is a point that Ronald Sider makes repeatedly. Moreover, the existence of such a loving community is indispensable before the church can bring a prophetic word to the society it serves. "The church should consist of communities of loving defiance."

Third, "the structures of secular society require revision". Repentance for personal sin is not enough. As the prophets made clear, we need to repent also for the structural evil in society; and any genuine repentance will lead to a serious attempt to change those structures which encourage the evil. If we neglect to do this, any personal and corporate attempts towards simple living will degenerate into "little more than a gloriously irrelevant ego-trip or proud pursuit of personal purity" (p. 178).

Many of the hard facts and statistics that Ronald Sider quotes are a trenchant *exposé* of the domestic and foreign policies of the United States. However, it would be both arrogant and foolish for those of us in other developed countries to dismiss what Sider has to say for this reason.

I profoundly believe that *this book contains the most vital challenge which faces the church of today*. It is one of the most searching and disquieting books I have ever read. It requires not only careful study, and, perhaps, some adaptation to the society in which we may live; it calls, above all, for immediate and sacrificial *action*, if we know anything of God's love in our hearts. It is useless calling Jesus "Lord, Lord", if we do not do what he tells us. It will not be easy. It will often be painful. But I am convinced that this practical expression of God's love for people, especially for the afflicted and oppressed, will bring about the greatest impact for Christ that the church could ever make in this present world.

"He who has an ear, let him hear what the Spirit says to the churches."

DAVID WATSON
St. Michael-le-Belfrey, York

Introduction

HUNGER AND STARVATION stalk the land. Famine is alive and well on planet earth. Millions of people die of starvation each year. Even the most conservative statistics reflect a horrifying situation. One billion people are starving or malnourished. Can overfed, comfortably clothed and luxuriously housed persons understand poverty? Can we truly feel what it is like to be a nine-year-old boy playing outside a village school which he cannot attend because his father is unable to afford the necessary books? (The books would cost less than my wife and I spent on some entertainment one evening during the writing of this book.) Can we really feel what it means for poverty-stricken parents to watch with helpless grief as their baby daughter dies of a common childhood disease because, like half of our global neighbours even today, they lack access to modern medicine? Probably not.

We can, however, make an attempt to understand. We can search for honest answers to questions such as these: How many people are actually hungry today? What are the effects of poverty? Tear-jerking rhetoric aside, how great is the gap between the rich and poor passengers on spaceship earth? And how does our affluence look in comparison with their poverty?

This book develops a biblical response. Part One sketches the setting with a brief overview of world poverty and the affluence of the Northern Hemisphere. The heart of our study is Part Two, "A Biblical Perspective on the Poor and Possessions." Part Three develops concrete suggestions for the individual, the church and society.

PART II

POOR LAZARUS & RICH CHRISTIANS

A BILLION HUNGRY NEIGHBOURS

SOMETIMES I THINK, "IF I DIE, I WON'T HAVE TO SEE MY CHILDREN SUFFERING AS THEY ARE." SOMETIMES I EVEN THINK OF KILLING MYSELF. SO OFTEN I SEE THEM CRYING, HUNGRY; AND THERE I AM, WITHOUT A CENT TO BUY THEM SOME BREAD. I THINK, "MY GOD, I CAN'T FACE IT! I'LL END MY LIFE. I DON'T WANT TO LOOK ANY MORE!" (IRACEMA DA SILVA, RESIDENT OF A SLUM IN BRAZIL)[1]

What does poverty really mean in daily life?

One way to try and answer this question is to list what a typical Western family would need to give up if they were to adopt the lifestyle of a typical family living among our billion hungry neighbours. Economist Robert Heilbroner has itemized the abandoned "luxuries".

We begin by invading the house of our imaginary Western family to strip it of its furniture. Everything goes: beds, chairs, tables, television set, lamps. We will leave the family with a few old blankets, a kitchen table, a wooden chair. Along with the bureaus go the clothes. Each member of the family may keep in his "wardrobe" his oldest suit or dress, a shirt or blouse. We will permit a pair of shoes for the head of the family, but none for the wife or children.

We move to the kitchen. The appliances have already been taken out, so we turn to the cupboards . . . The box of matches may stay, a small bag of flour, some sugar and salt. A few mouldy potatoes, already in the rubbish bin, must be hastily rescued, for they will provide much of tonight's meal. We will leave a handful of onions, and a dish of dried beans. All the rest we take away: the meat, the fresh vegetables, the canned goods . . .

Now we have stripped the house: the bathroom has been dismantled, the running water shut off, the electric wires taken out. Next we take away the house. The family can move to the toolshed . . .

Communications must go next. No more newspapers, magazines, books—not that they are missed, since we must take away our family's literacy as well. Instead, in our shantytown we will allow one radio . . .

Now government services must go. No more postman, no more firemen. There is a school, but it is three miles away and consists of two classrooms . . . There are, of course, no hospitals or doctors nearby. The nearest clinic is ten miles away and is tended by a midwife. It can be reached by bicycle, provided that the family has a bicycle, which is unlikely . . .

Finally, money. We will allow our family a cash hoard of £2.00. This will prevent our breadwinner from experiencing the tragedy of an Iranian peasant who went blind because he could not raise the £1.50 which he mistakenly thought he needed to receive admission to a hospital where he could have been cured.[2]

How many of our brothers and sisters confront that kind of grinding poverty today? Probably at least one billion people are as poor as this. They know hunger in a way that those of us in the West have never known, including those who can remember living through war-time and post-war rationing in Western Europe.

A study published in 1977 by the National Academy of Sciences of the United States indicated that "750 million people in the poorest nations live in extreme poverty with annual incomes of less than $75. Even in the middle income developing countries, World Bank estimates show about 170 million people at the extreme poverty level and hundreds of millions of others are subsisting at income levels less than one-third of their national averages."[3] The Food and Agriculture Organization (F.A.O.) of the U.N. estimated that at least 460 million people suffered from severe protein-energy malnutrition in 1970.[4] These figures excluded China and other Asian centrally-planned economies, for which comparable data was lacking. This estimate of at least 460 million severely malnourished people refers to an average year (1970). In years of drought or other calamities the numbers increase substantially. Indeed, the estimate refers to a period before the widespread bad weather and the drop in per capita food production that characterized 1972–74 in most of the developing countries of Africa and the Far East.[5] The consequent enormous food deficit of these developing countries where 80 per cent of the 460 million severely malnourished were already concentrated could not be met by increased imports, because by 1974, the price of cereals such as rice and wheat had tripled from the levels of early 1972, as a result of the worldwide grain shortage. Millions starved to death.

It was largely to try and deal with this disastrous situation that the World Food Conference was convened in November 1974. A special supplement to the U.N. publication *Development Forum* entitled 'Facts on Food' (November 1974) estimated that "half the world's population, 2000 million, is badly nourished". We will use a fairly conservative figure of 1 billion persons, who are malnourished in an average year, though this figure rises steeply at times of world food shortage such as 1972–74, and may be lower when crops, particularly those in the developing countries, are good, as has happened thankfully in 1975–77.

It is vital to remember that the effects of malnutrition do not disappear when a good crop comes along. The consequences of those years of extreme hunger will always be with tens of millions of children who survived, but who have already experienced severe irreversible damage to both brain and body during their childhood, and have weakened bodies highly vulnerable to disease because of their inadequate intake of calories and proteins.

THE THIRD AND FOURTH WORLDS Almost all these billion hungry people live in the Third and Fourth Worlds. Until recently, all countries that were not a part of the developed world, either capitalist or communist, were included in the developing Third World. But changes in the last decade, especially since the tripling of oil prices in 1973, require a new division into Third World and Fourth World countries.

India, Bangladesh and Pakistan and many African countries, including Ethiopia, Burundi, Chad, Tanzania and the Central African Republic, belong to the Fourth World. Typically less than one person in four is literate, though in India literacy is higher and the figure is about one in three. Infant mortality rates are up to ten times those in the developed world and population growth rates are higher. Unless there are major changes in international aid and trade, there is little prospect of a significant improvement in the appalling conditions for the people in these Fourth World countries. Hunger will continue to strike down millions.[6]

Some of the Third World countries have a somewhat brighter future. Most Latin American countries, and a few other countries in Asia and Africa, belong to the Third World. Some of these nations have experienced significant economic growth but this has frequently been of no help to the poor. Brazil and Mexico are classic examples.

In Brazil a military dictatorship strongly supported by the United States fostered economic growth at the rate of 10 per cent per year from 1968–74. But who profited? Even Brazil's own minister of finance admitted in 1972 that only 5 per cent of the people had benefited from the fantastic growth of the Brazilian economy. The Brazilian government did not challenge a 1974 study that showed that the real purchasing power of the poorest two-thirds of the people had declined by more than one-half in the preceding ten years. 40 per cent of Brazil's 110 million people suffer from malnutrition.[7]

In Brazil in 1970, 60 per cent of the people received less than 20 per cent of the country's total income.[8] From 1960 to 1970 the poorest 40 per cent saw their share of total income decline from 10 per cent to 8 per cent. But the wealthy elite of 5 per cent increased their share of total income from 29 per cent to 38 per cent.[9]

Things have probably become worse since then for the poor in Brazil, as they have suffered most from the problems experienced by the Brazilian economy since the rise in oil prices in 1973. Tragically, Brazil's rapid economic growth has been largely at the expense of the masses.

In Mexico where average per capita income grew in real terms by 3 per cent a year between 1950 and 1969, the richest 10 per cent pushed their share of total national income up from 49 per cent in 1950 to 51 per cent in 1969. Meanwhile the poor got less. In 1950, the bottom 40 per cent got 14 per cent of the income pie; by 1969 it was down to 11 per cent. The poorest 20 per cent saw their share of the income pie cut from 6 per cent to 4 per cent.[10] Unfortunately this sort of situation is found in many developing countries particularly in Latin America.

The tears and agony of all these people are captured in the words of Mrs. Alarin from the Philippines. The Alarin family of seven live in an eight-by-ten-foot room. Cooking utensils are their only furniture. Mr. Alarin makes forty pence on good days as an ice vendor. Several times a month, Mrs. Alarin stays up all night to make a coconut sweet which she sells on the street. Total income for her midnight toil: twenty-five pence. The family had not tasted meat for a month when Stan Mooneyham of World Vision visited Mrs. Alarin recently:

Tears washed her dark, sunken eye-sockets as she spoke: "I feel so sad when my children cry at night because they have no food. I know my life will never change. What can I do to solve my problems? I am so worried about the future of my children. I want them to go to school but how can we afford it? I am sick most of the time, but I can't go to the doctor because each visit costs two pesos [fifteen pence] and the medicine is extra. What can I do?" She broke down into quiet sobbing. I admit without shame that I wept with her.[11]

World poverty is a hundred million mothers weeping, like Mrs. Alarin, because they cannot feed their children.

What has led to our tragic situation?

THE BACKGROUND In the late 1960s the Green Revolution created widespread optimism. Agricultural specialists produced new strains of rice and wheat. As a result, poor countries like Mexico and India were almost self-sufficient in cereals by the early 1970s. However population growth had matched increased agricultural productivity,[12] so when there was a bad crop in 1972, as a result of bad weather conditions, hunger returned. Total world food production per capita declined substantially in 1972 for the first time since World War 2.

When oil prices tripled in 1973 farmers in the developing world could not afford the oil needed to run the irrigation pumps for the new strains of grain. Nor could they afford the necessary fertilizer which had increased in price by 150 per cent between 1972 and 1974.[13]

Tragically, rising affluence and poor harvests in North America, Europe, U.S.S.R. and Japan had also almost tripled the cost of grain for export in the same short period. When poor nations searched desperately for grain to feed their hungry masses in 1974, they had to pay two and a half times as much as two years earlier for every ton they needed. For some of the millions and millions of people who were already spending 80 per cent of their budget on food, there was only one possible outcome—starvation. Millions died.

The good harvests of 1975, 1976 and 1977, have greatly helped to redress this situation. But in early 1977, Keith Abercrombie, Deputy Director of the Policy Analysis Division of the Economic and Social Policy Department of the U.N.'s Food and Agriculture Organization summarized the longer term situation like this:

Although we really are pulling out of the immediate crisis that started in 1972, almost all of the longer term problems which faced the World Food Conference in November 1974 still remain. It would be very dangerous indeed to relapse into complacency again as did so many people during the green revolution years of 1967–1971. Even with the good results of 1975 and 1976 [and 1977], the longer term increase in food production in the developing countries is still far below the four per cent a year that is called for in the International Development Strategy for the Second Development Decade and which was reaffirmed by the World Food Conference.[14]

Unless there is a major international effort aimed specifically at improving the lot of the rural agricultural masses in the hungry nations, the lot of perhaps a billion persons will be the same in 1985 as it is today. The United Nations has predicted that short of such a major undertaking "it seems unlikely that the quantity of food per rural inhabitant could be greater in 1985 than it is today . . . and [certainly not enough] to make a significant impact on the general problem of rural poverty and hunger."[15]

FAMINE REDEFINED   Lester Brown, one of the specialists best informed on all aspects of the hunger crisis, points out that we must redefine famine.

One reason it is possible for the world's affluent to ignore such tragedies is that changes have occurred in the way that famine manifests itself. In earlier historical periods, . . . whole nations . . . experienced widespread starvation and death. Today the advancement in both national and international distribution systems has concentrated the effects of food scarcity among the world's poor, wherever they are.[16]

People with money can always buy food; famine affects only the poor.

When food scarcity triples the price of grain imports, as it did in 1972–74, middle and upper income persons in developing countries continue to eat. But millions of people who are already devoting 60 to 80 per cent of their income to food simply eat less and die sooner. Death is usually the result of a disease their underfed bodies could not resist.

Children are the first victims. In developing countries one child in four dies before the age of five. The infant mortality rate there is ten times higher than in developed countries. And half of these deaths are related to inadequate diets. In 1974 UNICEF estimated that 210 million children under five in the world were malnourished.[17] That means three malnourished children for every man, woman and child living in the U.K. and Australia!

Studies in Latin America, the World Bank reports, "show malnutrition to be either the primary cause of—or a major contributing factor in—50 to 75 per cent of the deaths of children under five years."[18]

Carolina Maria de Jesus helps one feel the terror and anguish endured by the poor in a land where they could have enough food. The feelings faithfully recorded daily on scraps of paper by this uneducated, brilliant woman who struggled to survive in the slums of Brazil's second largest city, Sâo Paulo, were published in a gripping diary called *Child of the Dark*.

Today I'm sad. I'm nervous. I don't know if I should start crying or start running until I fall unconscious. At dawn it was raining. I couldn't go out to get any money [she gathered junk each day to earn money for food] . . . I have a few tin cans and a little scrap that I'm going to sell to Senhor Manuel. When João came home from school, I sent him to sell the scrap. He got 13 cruzeiros. He bought a glass of mineral water: two cruzeiros. I was furious with him . . .

The children eat a lot of bread. They like soft bread but when they don't have it, they eat hard bread . . .

Oh Sâo Paulo! A queen that vainly shows her skyscrapers that are her crown of gold. All dressed up in velvet and silk but with cheap stockings underneath—the favela *[the slum].*

The money didn't stretch far enough to buy meat, so I cooked macaroni with a carrot. I didn't have any grease, it was horrible. Vera was the only one who complained yet asked for more.

"Mama, sell me to Dona Julita, because she has delicious food."[19]

Stanley Mooneyham of World Vision tells of a heart-rending visit to the home of Sebastian and Maria Nascimento, a poor Brazilian couple. The one-room, thatched lean-to had a sand floor. One stool, a charcoal hibachi and four cots covered with sacks partly filled with a bit of straw were the only furniture.

My emotions could scarcely take in what I saw and heard. The three-year-old twins, lying naked and unmoving on a small cot, were in the last act of their personal drama. Mercifully, the curtain was coming down on their brief appearance. Malnutrition was the villain. The two-year-old played a silent role, his brain already vegetating from marasmus, a severe form of malnourishment.

The father is without work. Both he and Maria are anguished over their existence, but they are too proud to beg. He tries to shine shoes. Maria cannot talk about their condition. She tries, but words just will not come. Her mother's love is deep and tender, and the daily deterioration of her children is more than she can bear. Tears must be the vocabulary of the anguished soul.[20]

Carolina's little girl need not have begged to be sold to a rich neighbour. While Sebastian and Maria's twins lay dying, there was still an abundance of food in the world. But it was not divided fairly. The well-to-do in Brazil had plenty to eat. Two hundred and ten million U.S. citizens were consuming enough food (partly because of high consumption of grain-fed livestock) to feed over one billion people in the poor countries!

This is how famine has been redefined, or rather, redistributed! It no longer inconveniences the rich and powerful. It strikes only the poor and powerless. Since the poor usually die quietly in relative obscurity, the rich of all nations comfortably ignore this kind of famine. But famine—redefined and redistributed—is alive and well. Even in good times, millions and millions of persons go to bed hungry. Their children's brains vegetate and their bodies succumb prematurely to disease.

Poverty means illiteracy, inadequate medical care, disease, brain damage. People in the West have enjoyed the security offered by modern medicine for so long that they assume it must now be available to all. But that is a tragic illusion. Population expert Lester Brown reminds us that "as of the mid-1970s, . . . an estimated one-third to one-half of mankind still lives without access to health services of any kind."[21]

INFANTS, BRAIN DAMAGE AND PROTEIN Lacking both food and medicine, the Third and Fourth Worlds have very high infant mortality rates. This is one important cause of the population explosion in underdeveloped nations. Because so many children die in infancy, a large family is desired to guarantee support for poor parents in old age.

Permanent brain damage caused by protein deficiency is one of the most devastating aspects of world poverty. 80 per cent of total brain development takes place between the moment of conception and the age of two. Adequate protein intake—precisely what at least 210 million malnourished children do not have—is necessary for proper brain development. A recent study in Mexico found that a group of severely malnourished children under five had an IQ thirteen points lower than a scientifically selected, adequately fed control group.[22]

Infant Mortality

(Number of deaths between birth and one year per 1,000 Live Births)

Sweden	9
U.K.	16
Australia	17
U.S.	17
West Germany	21
U.S.S.R.	28
Chile	78
Guatemala	81
Egypt	100
India	122
Pakistan	124
Rwanda	133
Malawi	142
Liberia	159

Source: U.N. Demographic year book 1975, pp. 153–157.
All figures refer to a year since 1968; for developed countries statistics refer to 1974.

Table 1

Medical science now agrees that severe malnutrition produces irreversible brain damage.

When a poor family runs out of food, the children suffer most. For the present, an inactive child is not as serious a problem as an inactive wage earner. But malnutrition produces millions of retarded children.

Little Marli, a happy six-year-old girl from Rio de Janeiro is just one of these. Little Marli looked normal in every way. Healthy. Happy. There was just one thing wrong with her. She couldn't learn. At first the teachers thought perhaps her difficulty was psychological, the result of neglect in a family of eleven children. Her younger sister had the same problem. But after careful obser-

vation and testing, it was evident that Marli, a child of Brazil's poor and wretched favelas [slums], was unable to learn because as an infant her malnourished body could not produce a healthy brain.[23]

No one knows how many poor children have suffered irreversible brain damage because of insufficient protein during childhood. But there were 210 million malnourished children in 1974. So the number of mental cripples like Marli must number millions.

Hunger, illiteracy, disease, brain damage, death. That's what world poverty means. At least one billion persons experience its daily anguish.

POPULATION The population explosion is another fundamental problem. Not until 1830 did the world have one billion persons. But then it took only a hundred years (1930) to add another billion. Within a mere thirty years another billion human beings appeared. The fourth billion arrived in only fifteen years (1975). By the year 2000 the world's population will have climbed to about seven billion persons.

Years Required to Add One Billion People

	years required	year reached
First billion	10,000 plus	1830
Second billion	100	1930
Third billion	30	1960
Fourth billion	15	1975
Fifth billion	11	1986
Sixth billion	9	1995

Source: Lester Brown, *In the Human Interest* (Oxford: Pergamon Press, 1976)

Table 2

The population explosion prompts some people to despair completely. The Environmental Fund ran an advertisement in 1976 in many newspapers including the *New York Times* and the *Wall Street Journal*. Drafted by William Paddock and Garrett Hardin, among others, the statement declared, "The world as we know it will likely be ruined before the year 2000 ... The momentum toward tragedy is at this moment so great that there is probably no way of halting it."[24]

Clearly the present rate of population growth cannot continue indefinitely. A population growing at the rate of 2·5 per cent per year (it is 2·7 per cent currently for all of Latin America) grows to nearly 12 times its current size in 100 years. If Latin America's population of 325 million were to increase at present rates for one hundred years, there would be more people in Latin America in 2075 than in the entire world today. (See Table 3)

Mexico's population is growing by over two million a year at the moment, so that in the ten years since the Olympic games in 1968, its population has grown from 46 million to 66 million, and if it carried on growing at that rate of 3·5 per cent till the year 2000, the population would have grown to 140 million people!

In considering the population growth issue it is important to remember that although Western developed nations have much lower population growth rates than developing nations now (see Table 4), the number of children per family in W. Europe+N. America was much higher in the latter half of the last century than the two or three children per family common now. Infant mortality rates were of course higher. However, despite this, family size and population growth then in the West were quite close to size and growth rates in many developing countries since the war. Affluence and decline in population growth seem to go together, in the long term anyway.

Along with the food crisis and the population explosion, a third set of complex, interrelated issues makes our dilemma even more desperate. How long can the earth sustain the present rate of industrialization? What will be the effect of the resulting pollution? When will we run out of natural resources (especially fossil fuels such as coal and oil)? In 1972 the Club of Rome (a group of elite, international corporation executives, technocrats and scholars) shocked the world with an answer based on a sophisticated, computerized analysis.[25]

Population increase over 25, 50 and 100 years.

Population growth rate per cent per year.	Ratio of projected population to current population. 25 years.	50 years.	100 years.
0·5	1·13	1·28	1·65
1·0	1·28	1·65	2·70
1·5	1·45	2·11	4·43
2·0	1·64	2·69	7·24
2·5	1·85	3·44	11·81
3·0	2·09	4·38	19·22
3·5	2·36	5·58	31·19

Table 3

Population growth rate per year (selected countries).

	1970-1975 Average annual rate of increase Population mid 76			Population mid 76
U.K.	0·2%	56·1m	India	2·1%	621m
West Germany	0·4%	62·1m	Mozambique	2·3%	9·3m
U.S.	0·8%	215·3m	Bangladesh	2·4%	76·1m
U.S.S.R.	0·9%	257m	Ethiopia	2·6%	28·6m
Japan	1·2%	112·3m	Nigeria	2·7%	65m
Canada	1·4%	23·1m	Brazil	3·0%	110m
China	1·4%	837m	Pakistan	3·0%	72·5m
Australia	1·5%	13·8m	Mexico	3·5%	62m
World	1·9%	4,015m			

Source: U.N. Demographic year book 1975, pp. 142–147.
Population growth rates. Estimates prepared by U.N. Population division for 1970–1975.
Population Estimates U.S. and World Development Agenda 1977, Overseas Development
Council (Praeger New York, London).

Table 4

Many valid objections have been raised against the computer model used in the *Limits to Growth* study and both the Club of Rome and the U.N. have recently published more optimistic projections.[26] But the issues which it spotlighted are still very much alive.

Although industrial production growth rates have come down since the oil crisis, the growth in Western industrial production and some growth in industrial production in developing countries will still place intolerable strains on the world's resources in the future. The debate taking place at the moment is about when this will happen, and which resources will be used up first, rather than if it will happen.

THE FUTURE AND OUR RESPONSE   The population explosion and the probable necessity of slowing industrialization (at least in the affluent nations) compound the difficulties involved in trying to divide the world's resources more justly. Not surprisingly, predictions of doomsday are legion. What are our future prospects?

No one can predict with any certainty what will happen in the next decade. Vast mushrooming famines in the poorer nations may tempt their leaders to unleash wars of unprecedented size and ferocity in a desperate attempt to demand a fairer share of the earth's resources. Such a prospect is not at all fantasy. In a recent book Professor Heilbroner predicts nuclear terrorism and "wars of redistribution". Heilbroner suggests that the world is like "an immense train, in which a few passengers, mainly in the advanced capitalist world, ride in first-class coaches, in conditions of comfort unimaginable to the enormously greater numbers crammed into the cattle cars that make up the bulk of the train's carriages".[27] As millions die and imminent starvation stares tens of millions of persons in the face, a country like India will have to seek some way out.

There seems little doubt that some nuclear capability will be in the hands of the major underdeveloped nations certainly within the next few decades and perhaps much sooner . . . I will suggest that it may be used as an instrument of blackmail to force the developed world to undertake a massive transfer of wealth to the poverty-

stricken world . . . "Wars of redistribution" may be the only way by which the poor nations can hope to remedy their condition.[28]
Less than a year after Heilbroner's book appeared, India exploded her first nuclear bomb.

The result of such a confrontation could only be ghastly bloodshed on a scale never before seen in human history. We would undoubtedly use our vast military might to defend our unfair share of the world's goods. Tens—perhaps even hundreds—of millions would die.

Such an outcome seems too horrible to contemplate. But realism demands that we honestly face the fact that unless the affluent quarter of the world makes fundamental changes quickly, wars of unprecedented size and ferocity are quite probable.

Stanley Mooneyham, President of World Vision, a large evangelical relief and development agency, helps us understand why:
They have suffered long with "aid" that isn't, with discriminatory trade policies, with the rape of their resources.[29]
U.S. Senator Mark Hatfield concurs. He has recently warned,
The greatest threat to this nation [the United States] and the stability of the entire world is hunger. It's more explosive than all the atomic weaponry possessed by the big powers. Desperate people do desperate things, and remember that nuclear fission is now in the hands of even the developing nations.[30]
Professor Georg Borgstrom, world-renowned specialist in food science and nutrition, fears that "the rich world is on a direct collision course with the poor of the world . . . We cannot survive behind our Maginot Line of missiles and bombs."[31]
But the probability is that we would try. And the result could only be war and carnage, repression and totalitarianism.

What will Christians do in such a time? Will we dare to insist that the God revealed in Scripture is always at work seeking to "set at liberty those who are oppressed" (Lk. 4:18)? Will Christians have the courage to seek justice for the poor even if that means prison? Where will you and I stand? With the starving or the overfed? With poor Lazarus or the rich man? Most of the rich countries are white and at least nominally Christian. What an ironic tragedy if the white, affluent,

"Christian" minority in the world continue to amass wealth while hundreds of millions of people hover on the edge of starvation!

One popular fundamentalist newsletter (with a circulation of over 60,000) has called on Christians to stockpile new dried foods. In a most ingenious combination of apocalyptic piety and slick salesmanship, a recent edition quoted several "Bible scholars" to prove that some Christians will live through the tribulation. And the conclusion? Since one cannot be absolutely certain where one will be during the tribulation, one ought to purchase a seven-year supply of reserve foods for a couple of thousand dollars![32]

In an Age of Hunger most Christians (regardless of theological labels) will be severely tempted to succumb to the liberal heresy of following current cultural and societal values rather than biblical truth.[33] Society will offer demonically convincing justification for enjoying our affluence and forgetting about a billion hungry neighbours.

But if the Christ of Scripture is our Lord, then we will refuse to be squeezed into the mould of our affluent, sinful culture. In an Age of Hunger Christians of necessity must be radical nonconformists. But nonconformity is painful. Only if we are thoroughly grounded in the scriptural view of possessions, wealth and poverty will we be capable of living an obedient lifestyle.

THE AFFLUENT MINORITY

I USED TO THINK, WHEN I WAS A CHILD, THAT CHRIST MIGHT HAVE BEEN EXAGGERATING WHEN HE WARNED ABOUT THE DANGERS OF WEALTH. TODAY I KNOW BETTER. I KNOW HOW VERY HARD IT IS TO BE RICH AND STILL KEEP THE MILK OF HUMAN KINDNESS. MONEY HAS A DANGEROUS WAY OF PUTTING SCALES ON ONE'S EYES, A DANGEROUS WAY OF FREEZING PEOPLE'S HANDS, EYES, LIPS, AND HEARTS.[1] [DOM HELDER CAMARA]

The north-south division is the most dangerous division in the world today. With one or two exceptions, the rich countries are in the Northern Hemisphere, and the poor countries are in the south. North America, Europe, Russia and Japan are an affluent Northern aristocracy. Our standard of living is at least as luxurious in comparison with that of a billion hungry neighbours as was the lifestyle of the medieval aristocracy in comparison with their serfs.

HOW WEALTHY ARE WE? One way of trying to measure the relative wealth of people in the developed and developing world is by using the Gross National Product (GNP) of a country. GNP is the sum of all goods and services produced annually by an economy, after allowance is made for payments of profits and interest to foreign owners of capital, and receipts on this account from overseas. GNP per capita can therefore provide a comparison between developed and developing countries, but it does have several serious problems.

1. GNP and GNP per capita say nothing about the distribution of income, which as we saw in Chapter 1 can mean that a large proportion of income and growth in income are concentrated in a small proportion of the population.

2. Developing countries are usually largely rural and have non-monetary economies (subsistence farming means only a small proportion of output is marketed).

3. The most serious of these problems though is that we are interested not in how much per capita income a person has, but how much food, clothing, health care, etc., they can obtain with that income. Per capita income would be a very useful measure if the prices of goods and services were virtually the same throughout the world, but they are not. Prices are not equalized by world trade, partly because some goods and services, such as haircuts, cannot be traded and for other reasons, such as transportation, distribution costs, trade restrictions, etc.

Even the prices of some goods between countries where there are virtually no barriers to trade, such as the U.K. and France and Germany, are far from equalized (witness the vast number of French and Germans buying goods in U.K. shops). Hence it is not very realistic to compare total output in the U.K. at U.K. prices and total output in Bangladesh at Bangladesh prices!

Some development specialists have tried to take these differences into account and have estimated that "differences in income per head between the poor and rich countries were around 1:2 at the beginning of the 19th century; they are around 1:40 today in nominal or around 1:20 in real terms".[2]

In 1975 Professor Irving Kravis, specialist in income comparisons at the University of Pennsylvania, published a massive, painstaking comparison of total output and real purchasing power in different countries. He concluded that real income per person in the United States in 1970 was fourteen times that of India and seventeen times that of Kenya.[3]

A conservative estimate might be that the real income in goods and services of the average person in the Western developed world is about TEN TIMES that of the average person in a developing country, and hundreds of millions are of course below that average. This statistic applies just as much to the U.K., where, despite economic problems, the standard of living in real terms and quality of life are still amongst the highest in the Western world. In 1977 the Overseas Development Council of the U.S.A. published a 'Physical Quality of Life Index' (P.Q.L.I.) as a way of measuring the development of a country, using three basic statistics, infant mortality, literacy and life expectancy. Using this index it rated the U.K. slightly higher than both the U.S.A. and West Germany.[4]

There are many ways of showing our incredible affluence in the West relative to that of developing countries but undoubtedly the most striking measure of the gap between rich and poor is our consumption of the most basic commodity of all—food. Table 5 shows that Europeans consume two and a half times as much cereal per person as do the people in the developing countries, although cereals such as rice are the staple diet of almost all the developing countries.

Average Annual Per Capita Cereal Consumption (pounds) (Direct and Indirect), 1965–66 and 1972–74[5]

	1964–66 average	1972–74 average
United States	1,600	1,850
U.S.S.R.	1,105	1,435
European Community	900	1,000
Japan	530	620
China	420	430
Developing countries (excluding China)	370	395

Source: Organization for Economic Cooperation and Development.

Table 5

The grain consumption figures of the E.E.C. and Japan are lower than those of the U.S.A. and U.S.S.R. partly because fish, particularly in Japan, play a larger role in diets there than they do in the U.S.A. and U.S.S.R.

The major reason for the glaring difference in cereal consumption between the rich and poor nations is that we Europeans and other affluent people eat much of our grain indirectly—via grain-fed livestock and fowl. See Table 6.

Annual Grain Consumption by main types of use 1970

In 1970, grain used as feed for livestock in the developed countries totalled 371·5 million metric tons—which was larger than that consumed as food and feed in developing countries though they had a population two-thirds larger!

	Developed countries (million metric tons)	Developing Market Economies (million metric tons)
Food	160·9	303·7
Feed	371·5	35·6
Other uses	84·9	46·4
Total	617·3	385·7
Population (1970)	1,072 million	1,750 million
Kg per capita	576	220

Source: Adapted from p. 184 *U.S. and World Development. Agenda 1977*, Overseas Development Council (Praeger; London, New York).

Table 6

It takes many pounds of grain to produce just one pound of beef. According to the Economic Research Service of the U.S. Department of Agriculture, a steer in a feed lot gains one pound of edible meat for every thirteen pounds of grain consumed! But the animal also spends time on the range eating grass. (But it does not spend as much time on the range as in the past. On November 28, 1974 the *New York Times* reported that in the 1940s only one-third of all beef was grain-fed. By 1970, 82 per cent of all cattle slaughtered came in from feed lots where they were fed grain.) The U.S. Department of Agriculture reports that when the total life of the animal is considered, each pound of edible beef represents seven pounds of grain.[6] That means that in addition to all the grass, hay and other food involved, it also took seven pounds of grain to produce a typical pound of beef purchased in the supermarket. Although these are U.S. figures, figures for other developed countries such as the U.K. are broadly comparable, and the trend towards grain feeding of livestock has been true of all developed countries. Fortunately, the conversion rates for chicken and pork are lower: two or three to one for chicken and three or four to one for pork. Beef is the Rolls-Royce of meat products. Should we move to a Mini?

It is because of this high level of meat consumption that the rich minority of the world devours such an unfair share of the world's available food. Whereas we eat most of our grain indirectly via meat, people in the poor countries eat almost all of their grain directly. The United Nations reports that livestock in the rich countries eat as much grain as do all the people of India and China (over 1,400 million people).

While lack of food destroys millions in poor lands, too much food devastates millions in affluent countries. According to the American Medical Association, 40 per cent of the U.S. population is overweight,[8] and although the figure for the U.K. is lower than this obesity is a growing problem even here.

The percentage of disposable income spent on food in different countries provides another stark comparison. In the United States it is a mere 17 per cent. In India 67 per cent.

Agony and anguish are concealed in the simple statistics of Table 7. If one is spending 17 per cent of one's disposable income on food, a 50 per cent increase in food costs is an irrita-

Percentage of Disposable Income Spent on Food			
United States	17%	Indonesia	50%
Great Britain	22%	Peru	52%
Japan	23%	Zaire (Congo)	62%
Soviet Union	38%	India	67%

Source: Simon, *Bread for the World*, p. 40.

Table 7

tion. But if one is already spending 67 per cent of one's income on food to buy just enough to live on, a 50 per cent increase means starvation.

The percentage of disposable income spent on food is one way of measuring development. The poorer a person is, the larger the proportion spent on food. This of course applies within countries as well as between countries. The 67 per cent figure for India is only an average, and of course many Indians are spending an even higher proportion of their income on food.

Despite the much higher proportion of their income that people in developing countries spend on food, their nutritional levels are much lower than their counterparts in the affluent developing countries. Table 8 gives the average per capita intake of calories, a measurement of the energy supply, and grams of protein, for selected countries.

The facts are clear. North Americans, Europeans, Russians and Japanese devour an incredibly unjust share of the world's available food. Whether measured in terms of real income or food consumption, we are many, many times more affluent than the poor majority of our sisters and brothers. By any objective criterion this 25 per cent of the world's people is an incredibly rich aristocracy living among a vast, hungry proletariat. Surely one of the most astounding things, therefore, about this affluent minority is that we honestly think we barely have enough to survive in modest comfort.

Christians earning £4,000 a year or more have been heard to complain that they are poor! In summer 1977, a leader of one of Britain's professions said that his members were "worrying themselves sick" on how they could manage on £8,500 a year. To the vast majority of the world's people such statements would be unintelligible—or very dishonest. To be sure, we do need £4,000 a year (which is above average earnings for the U.K. in 1977) or even more if we are going to run a car, have a comfortable suburban home full of "labour-saving devices", and demand some new clothes every year. Most Christians in the West have come to expect precisely that, but it is hardly life at the edge of poverty. In fact it is undreamed-of luxury to hundreds of millions of our brothers and sisters in the developing world.

Food Supply in Individual Countries (including Fish) 1969–71 average.

	Per caput daily Dietary Energy supply Calories	Protein supply Grams
U.S.A.	3330	106
Australia	3280	108
U.S.S.R.	3280	101
West Germany	3220	89
U.K.	3190	92
Canada	3180	101
Japan	2510	79
China	2170	60
Pakistan	2160	56
India	2070	52
Zaire	2060	33
Rwanda	1960	58
Bolivia	1900	46
Bangladesh	1840	40
Haiti	1730	39
Upper Volta	1710	59

In assessing these figures, it should be noted that:

1. Calorie requirements are related (though not proportional) to body weights, and these are generally lower in developing countries than in the developed world.

2. A population with a high proportion of children (as is the case with most developing countries in Asia and Africa) will require less calories per head than a population with a greater percentage of adults.

3. Environmental factors affect calorie needs; less calories are required to maintain body temperature in a warm climate than in a cold one.

4. Per capita figures often conceal the fact that large sections of the population may well be receiving substantially less than this. This happens mainly because of income distribution differences.

5. The figures refer to 1969–71 when per capita food production in developing countries in Africa and Asia was much higher than in 1972–74.

6. Physical work increases calorie requirements, and in developing countries most people are employed in physically strenuous agricultural labour, which increases calorie needs relative to the more sedentary occupations that are normal in the developed world.

Source: Adapted from pp. 105–6, *The State of Food and Agriculture 1975* (F.A.O. Rome 1976).

Table 8

Constant, seductive advertising helps to create this destructive delusion. Advertisers regularly con us into believing that we genuinely need one luxury after another. We are convinced that we must keep up with or even go one better than our neighbours. So we buy another dress, suit or pair of shoes and thereby force up the standard of living. The ever more affluent standard of living is the god of twentieth-century Western people and the ad-man is its prophet.

The purpose of advertising no longer is primarily to inform. It is to create desire. "CREATE MORE DESIRE" shrieked one inch-high headline for an unusually honest ad in the *New York Times*. It continued: "Now, as always, profit and growth stem directly from the ability of salesmanship to create more desire."[9] Luxurious houses in *Country Life*, *Ideal Home* or *Homes and Gardens* make one's perfectly adequate house shrink by comparison into a dilapidated, tiny cottage in need of immediate renovation. The advertisements for the new season's fashions make our almost new dresses and suits from previous years look shabby and positively old-fashioned.

We are bombarded by costly, manipulative advertising at every turn. The average Briton watches television containing 5–10,000 commercials every year.[10]

In 1977, £1,500 million was spent in the U.K. on advertising "to convince us that Jesus was wrong about the abundance of possessions".[11]

Luxuries are renamed necessities by advertising. Our postman recently delivered an elegant brochure complete with glossy photographs of exceedingly expensive homes. The brochure announced the seductive lie that *Architectural Digest* would help one quench "man's passionate *need* for beauty and *luxury*" (my emphasis). Supposedly, we "need" luxuries!

Sometimes advertising overkill is hilarious. An evangelical book discount house recently created this pious, promotional gem: "Your mouth is going to water, and your soul is going to glow, when you feast your eyes on the bargains we have been providentially provided for your benefit this month." (I promptly ordered books worth twenty-four dollars! My library is one of my near idols.)

PROMISES, PROMISES Perhaps the most devastating and most demonic part of advertising is that it attempts to persuade us that material possessions will bring joy and fulfilment. "That happiness is to be attained through limitless material acquisition is denied by every religion and philosophy known to man, but is preached incessantly by every commercial on television."[12] Advertisers promise that their products will satisfy our deepest needs and inner longings for love, acceptance, security and sexual fulfilment. The right deodorant, they promise, will bring acceptance and friendship. The newest toothpaste or shampoo will make one irresistible. A house or bank account will guarantee security and love.

Examples are everywhere. A bank in Washington, D.C., recently advertised for new savings accounts with the question: "Who's gonna love you when you're old and grey?" Our savings bank sponsors a particularly enticing ad: "Put a little love away. Everybody needs a penny for a rainy day. Put a little love away." Those words are unbiblical, heretical, demonic. They teach the Big Lie of our secular, materialistic society. But the words and music are so seductive that they dance through my head hundreds of times.

If no one paid any attention to these lies, they would be harmless. But that is impossible. Advertising has a powerful effect on all of us. It shapes the values of our children. Many people in our society truly believe that more possessions will bring acceptance and happiness.

In a sense we pay too little attention to advertisements. Most of us think that we ignore them. But in fact they seep into our unconscious minds. We experience them instead of analysing them. We should examine their blatant lies and then laugh hilariously at their preposterous promises. John V. Taylor has suggested that Christian families ought to adopt the slogan "Who Are You Kidding?" and shout it in unison every time a commercial appears on the screen.[13] An alternative is simply to turn down the sound whenever a commercial break comes on. Fortunately in Britain the commercial breaks are much less frequent than in America, though each commercial break is longer, and they occur on only one of the three channels.

Theologian Patrick Kerans has recently argued that our society's commitment to a growth economy and an ever-increasing standard of living promoted by constant advertising is really a sell-out to the Enlightenment. During the eighteenth century, Western society decided that the scientific method would shape our relationship to reality. Since only quantitative criteria of truth and value were acceptable, more intangible values such as community, trust and friendship became less important. Unlike friendship and justice, GNP can be measured. The result is our competitive, growth economy where winning and economic success (and they are usually the same) are all-important.[14]

The result, if Kerans is correct, can only be social disintegration. If our basic social structures are built on the heretical suppositions of the Enlightenment that the scientific method is the only way to truth and value, and if Christianity is true, then our society must eventually collapse.

Advertising itself contains a fundamental inner contradiction.[15] Christians know that affluence does not guarantee love, acceptance and joy. But advertising promises them to those who strive feverishly for more gadgets and bigger bank accounts. Given our inherent bent for idolatry, advertising is so demonically powerful and convincing that most people persist in their fruitless effort to quench their thirst for meaning and fulfilment with an ever-rising river of possessions.

The result is inner, agonizing distress and undefined dissatisfaction and external, structural injustice. Our affluence fails to satisfy our restless hearts. And it also helps to deprive one billion hungry neighbours of badly needed food and resources. Will we affluent Christians have the courage and faithfulness to learn how to be unconformed to this world's seductive, satanic advertising?

HOW GENEROUS ARE WE? In 1975 the Organization for Economic Cooperation and Development (an organization of rich nations) underlined the contrast between growing wealth and declining foreign aid. In 1961–62 developed countries as a whole gave 0·52 per cent of total GNP in economic foreign aid. By 1974 it had declined to a mere 0·33 per cent (one-third of one per cent). But the economies of developed countries grew at an annual rate of 3·5 per cent per year during the past fifteen years. The OECD report concludes with the following statement:

This means that, at the end of a ten-year period, the resources available per person [*in developed countries*] *had increased by 41 per cent. To have reached the 0·7 per cent target* [*for development aid*] *from a starting point of 0·5 per cent would have reduced the* increase *in resources available for other purposes only marginally —from 41 to 40·5 per cent.* [16]

But developed nations would not spare a mere 1/82 of their *increase*!

Table 9 sets out the flows of official development assistance (ODA) from various developed countries. Column 1 represents the traditional league table of donors' ODA expressed as a per cent of GNP. From this it can be seen that only three countries met the modest U.N. target that ODA should be at least 0·7 per cent of GNP. Although the volume of aid is obviously very important, its effectiveness in helping the development of those in greatest need should be the prime concern.

This will be determined by how it is given (multilateral or bilateral); the terms of the aid (grants or loans); the type of aid (technical assistance, the provision of goods); the countries it is given to and whom and how it helps in those countries. ODA can be given either bilaterally, country to country or multilaterally through international institutions such as the U.N. organizations, the World Bank and the regional development banks, and the E.E.C. Column 2 shows the proportion of bilateral aid in each country's aid programme; in ten out of the fourteen countries it is between 66 and 86 per cent and because a country obviously has far more control over its bilateral aid policy, an analysis of its bilateral programme will reflect its aid strategy.

One of the saddest legacies of post-war "aid" from rich countries was that so much "aid" was in the form of loans, often with interest, and this has built up a huge burden of debt for many developing countries, and servicing this debt has caused them considerable economic difficulty. Now, however, some rich countries are giving their new aid, at least to the

43

Official Development Assistance (ODA) net from selected developed countries—1976

Country	Col 1 Total ODA as % of GNP	Col 2 % of ODA given as Bilateral aid	Col 3 Grant aid as a % of Bilateral ODA	Col 4 Technical Assistance as a % of Bilateral ODA	Col 5 % of Bilateral ODA given to poorer countries (all LLDCs and/or MSAs)	Col 6 % of GNP given as bilateral ODA to the poorer countries
Sweden	0·82	66	94	12	56	0·30
Netherlands	0·82	69	77	36	40	0·22
Norway	0·71	49	100	24	68	0·24
France	0·62	86	89	57	25	0·13
Denmark	0·56	55·	56	27	63	0·19
Belgium	0·51	67	89	62	30	0·10
Canada	0·46	60	63	13	59	0·16
New Zealand	0·43	82	95	35	14	0·05

Australia	0·42	83	100	21	10	0·04
UK	0·38	70	97	40	56	0·15
West Germany	0·31	75	49	42	48	0·11
US	0·25	66	59	14	35	0·06
Japan	0·20	68	25	14	32	0·04
Italy	0·13	29	58	42	17	0·01

Sources: *Development Co-operation, 1977 Review*, Organization for Economic Cooperation and Development. Table A.10, pp. 174–75.
Col 5: *British Aid Statistics, 1972–76*, Ministry of Overseas Development (H.M.S.O.).
Table 48, p 121.

Table 9

poorer countries, on grant, i.e. gift, terms. The U.K. has been doing this since 1975, and on July 31st 1978 announced that it was writing off debts of over £900m due from seventeen of the world's poorest countries. In assessing the figures in Column 3 it should be remembered that net bilateral loans may be small, and therefore grant aid a large percentage of bilateral ODA, because a country is receiving substantial capital repayments on previous loans thus leaving a small net loan figure rather than because it is giving nearly all grants in its current bilateral programme.

Aid is usually given in the form of Technical Assistance (TA) which is concerned mainly with the transfer of skills and the provision of advice to developing countries, and the supply of goods to assist the country's development or sometimes relief. Column 4 shows the proportion of TA in bilateral aid, with countries in Western Europe generally giving much more of their aid in the form of TA than the other rich countries.

The final issue the table deals with is whether bilateral ODA is going to the poorer countries (Column 5). There are several ways of trying to define the poorer countries, but a generally accepted definition is those countries classified by the U.N. as LLDC (least developed)—twenty-nine countries—or MSA (most seriously affected)—forty-five countries—by the rise in the price of oil, food and other commodities after 1974. All but five of the LLDC's are also MSA. So the total number of countries that are classified either MSA or LLDC is fifty. Thirty of them are in Africa, with a combined population in 1976 of about 230 million, five in the Caribbean, Central and South America with a population of 20 million, and the other fifteen are in Asia Pacific with a population of 870 million, making a total population of 1,120 million in the fifty countries. Considering the large number of these countries, their geographical spread and above all their enormous total population, which means they encompass the overwhelming majority of the world's poorest billion people outside the centrally planned economies, column 5 of Table 9 makes depressing reading. Only five of the fourteen rich countries gave more than half their bilateral aid to these fifty countries.

In the case of Australia and New Zealand, almost all their

bilateral aid goes to the Pacific where only one country, Western Samoa, is classified MSA or LLDC. In fact 70 per cent of Australia's total bilateral programme went to the 3 million people in Papua New Guinea. Belgium's figure is distorted by the fact that over 40 per cent of her bilateral programme goes to Zaire (pop. 25m), which despite having a per capita GNP of less than India or Pakistan, is not classified as an LLDC or MSA and has the lowest GNP per capita of countries not in the LLDC or MSA group. If Zaire were included in the poorer countries group Belgium would be giving over 70 per cent of her bilateral aid to the poorer countries. The low figure for the U.S. in column 5 is attributable to the substantial decline in real terms of its aid programme to South Asia and a substantial increase to one-third of ODA to countries in the Near East mainly in the form of "security supporting assistance" and to a lesser extent food aid. One country with a population of $3\frac{1}{2}$ million in this area received nearly a quarter of the total U.S. bilateral aid budget.

But it is in the French bilateral aid programme that the most surprising things turn up. France has long given the highest proportion of GNP in ODA out of the seven largest countries in the rich non-communist world, but as column 2 shows most of it is bilateral aid. Of this massive bilateral aid programme, second only to the U.S., only 25 per cent went to the over 1,100 million people in the fifty poorest countries. Nearly twice that, 45 per cent of the bilateral programme went to under $1\frac{1}{2}$ million people in Reunion, Guadeloupe, Martinique and French Guiana and Polynesia. Column 6, which is the product of columns 1, 2, 5, gives perhaps a slightly more accurate picture with an allowance made for multilateral contributions, of how generous we really are to the 1,100 million people who live in the poorest countries of the world, and this is before taking into account perhaps the most important question of all. Even if the aid goes to the poorest countries, does it help the development of the poorest 30–40 per cent of the people in those countries as they are surely our target group?

RATIONALISING OUR AFFLUENCE It would be impossible for the rich minority to live with themselves if they did not invent plausible justifications. These rationalizations take many forms. Analyzing a few of the most common may help us spot each year's new models.

In the last few years, concepts such as "triage"[17] and "lifeboat ethics" have become increasingly popular. Dr. Garrett Hardin, a distinguished biologist at the University of California at Santa Barbara, has provoked impassioned, widespread debate with his provocative articles on "lifeboat ethics".[18] He argues that we should not help the poor countries with food or aid. Each rich country is a lifeboat that will survive only if it refuses to waste its very limited resources on the hungry masses swimming in the water around it. If we eat together today, we will all starve together tomorrow. Furthermore, since poor countries "irresponsibly" permit unrestrained population growth, starvation is the only way to check the ever-growing number of hungry mouths. Hence, increased aid merely postpones the day of reckoning. When it comes, our aid will only have preserved even more persons for ultimate starvation. Therefore it is ethically correct to help them learn the hard way—by letting them starve now!

Hardin ignores recent data which show that poor countries can (and have) cut population growth fairly rapidly if, instead of investing in advanced technology and industrial development, they concentrate on improving the lot of the poor masses. If the poor masses have a secure food supply, access to some (relatively inexpensive) health services and modest educational opportunities, population growth tends to decline quickly. Lester Brown summarizes recent findings:

There is new striking evidence that in an increasing number of poor countries . . . birth rates have dropped sharply despite relatively low per capita income . . . Examination of societies as different as China, Barbados, Sri Lanka, Uruguay, Taiwan, The Indian Punjab, Cuba and South Korea suggests a common factor. In all these countries, a large portion of the population has gained access to modern social and economic services—such as education, employment, and credit systems . . . There is increasing evidence that the very strategies which cause the greatest improvement in the welfare of the entire population also have the greatest effect on reducing population growth.[19]

48

The right kind of aid—focussed especially on promoting labour-intensive, agricultural development using intermediate technology[20] will help check population growth. Hardin's ghastly thesis suggests doing nothing at a time when the right kind of action could probably avoid disaster.

Another omission in Hardin's thesis is even more astonishing. He totally ignores the fact that the ever increasing affluence among the rich minority is one of the fundamental causes of the present crisis. It is simply false to suggest that there is not enough food to feed everyone. There is enough—if it is more evenly distributed. In 1970 the United Nations estimated that it would take only 12 million additional tons of grain per year to provide 260 extra calories per day to the 460 million people suffering from malnutrition. That is only 30 per cent of what the U.S. feeds its livestock.[21] In a world where the rich minority feed more grain to their livestock than all the people in India and China eat, it is absurd and immoral to talk of the necessity of letting selected hungry nations starve. The boat in which the rich sail is not an austerely equipped lifeboat. It is a lavishly stocked luxury liner.

Hardin's proposal, of course, is also unrealistic. Hungry nations left to starve would not disappear in submissive silence. India is one of the nations frequently nominated for this dubious honour. As indicated before, a nation with nuclear weapons would certainly not tolerate such a decision![22]

A second rationalization has a pious ring to it. Some evangelical Christians argue that they must adopt an affluent lifestyle in order to evangelise wealthy persons. But that is highly questionable.

Where does valid justification end and rationalization begin? We must avoid simplistic legalism. Christians certainly ought to live in the suburbs as well as the inner city. But those who defend an affluent lifestyle on the basis of a call to witness to the rich must ask themselves hard questions: How much of my affluent lifestyle is directly related to my witnessing to rich neighbours? (For people who go out to work much of their witness is to those they work with. A humbler lifestyle may convince others that our Christian faith really does mean something especially when it affects even our pocket!)

How much of it could I abandon for the sake of Christ's poor and still be able to witness effectively? Indeed how much of it *must* I abandon in order to faithfully proclaim the biblical Christ who clearly taught that failure to feed the poor entails eternal damnation (Mt. 25:45–46)?

In the coming decades rationalizations for our affluence will be legion. They will be popular and persuasive. "Truly, I say to you, it will be hard for a rich man to enter the kingdom of heaven" (Mt. 19:23). But all things are possible with God—if we will hear and obey his Word. If there is any ray of hope for the future, it is in the possibility that growing numbers of affluent Christians will dare to allow the Bible to shape their relationship to a billion sons and daughters of poor Lazarus. The next four chapters will develop a biblical perspective on poverty and possessions.

PART II

A BIBLICAL PERSPECTIVE ON THE POOR & POSSESSIONS

Martin Luther once said that "if you preach the Gospel in all aspects with the exception of the issues which deal specifically with your time you are not preaching the Gospel at all".[1]

Luther's comment relates directly to the findings of a recent scholarly study. Social scientists examined the factors that shape attitudes on matters related to the development of the poor nations. They discovered that religion plays no significant role at all! Those with deep religious beliefs are no more concerned about assistance and development for the poor than are persons with little or no religious commitment.[2]

Western Christians have failed to declare God's perspective on the plight of our billion hungry neighbours—surely one of the most pressing issues of our time.

But I refuse to believe that this failure must inevitably continue. I believe there are millions of Christians in affluent lands who care more about Jesus than anything else in the world. There are millions of Christians who will take any risk, make any sacrifice, forsake any treasure, if they see clearly that God's Word demands it. That is why part two, "A Biblical Perspective on the Poor and Possessions," is the most important section of our study.

GOD & THE POOR

HE WHO IS KIND TO THE POOR LENDS TO THE LORD. [PROV. 19:17] I KNOW THAT THE LORD MAINTAINS THE CAUSE OF THE AFFLICTED, AND EXECUTES JUSTICE FOR THE NEEDY. [PS. 140:12]

What is the biblical approach to possessions and poverty?

Is God biased in favour of the poor? Some theologians have recently said yes.[1] The question, however, is ambiguous. Does it mean that God desires the salvation of poor people more than the salvation of the rich? Does it mean that God and his people treat the poor so conspicuously differently from the way the rich and powerful normally treat them that we can say that God seems to have a special concern for the poor and oppressed? Is God on the side of the poor in a way that he is not on the side of the rich?

We can answer these questions about God's "bias" toward the poor only after we have searched for biblical answers to five related questions: (1) What concern for the poor did God disclose at those pivotal points (especially the Exodus, the destruction of Israel and Judah, and the Incarnation) where he acted in history to reveal himself? (2) In what sense does God identify with the poor? (3) How significant is the fact that God very frequently chooses to work through the poor and oppressed? (4) What does the Bible mean by the constantly recurring teaching that God destroys the rich and exalts the poor? (5) Does God command his people to have a special concern for the poor?

PIVOTAL POINTS OF REVELATION HISTORY The Bible clearly and repeatedly teaches a fundamental point that we have often overlooked. At the crucial moments when God displayed his mighty acts in history to reveal his nature and will, God *also* intervened to liberate the poor and oppressed.

1. *The Exodus.* God displayed his power at the Exodus in order to free oppressed slaves! When he called Moses at the burning bush, God's intention was to end suffering and injustice: "I have seen the affliction of my people who are in Egypt, and have heard their cry because of their taskmasters; I know their sufferings, and I have come down to deliver them out of the hand of the Egyptians" (Ex. 3:7–8). Nor does this text in any way reflect an isolated perspective on the great event of the Exodus. Each year at the harvest festival, the Israelites repeated a liturgical confession celebrating the way God had acted to free a poor, oppressed people.

A wandering Aramean was my father; and he went down into Egypt and sojourned there ... And the Egyptians treated us harshly, and afflicted us, and laid upon us hard bondage. Then we cried to the LORD the God of our fathers, and the LORD heard our voice, and saw our affliction, our toil, and our oppression; and the LORD brought us out of Egypt with a mighty hand. (Deut. 26:5–8)

The God of the Bible cares when people enslave and oppress others. At the Exodus he acted to end economic oppression and bring freedom to slaves.

Now of course the liberation of oppressed slaves was not God's only purpose in the Exodus. God also acted because of his covenant with Abraham, Isaac and Jacob. He wanted to create a special people to whom he could reveal himself.[2] The liberation of a poor, oppressed people, however, was right at the heart of God's design. The following passage discloses God's multifaceted purpose in the Exodus:

Moreover I have heard the groaning of the people of Israel whom the Egyptians hold in bondage and I have remembered my covenant [with Abraham, Isaac and Jacob] ... I will bring you out from under the burdens of the Egyptians, and I will deliver you from their bondage, and I will redeem you with an outstretched arm and with great acts of judgement, and I will take you for my people,

*and I will be your God; and you shall know that I am the LORD
your God, who has brought you out from under the burdens of the
Egyptians.* (Ex. 6:5–7)

Yahweh wanted his people to know him as the One who freed
them from slavery and oppression.

The preamble to the Ten Commandments, probably the
most important portion of the entire law for Israel, begins with
this same revolutionary truth. Before he gives the two tables
of the law, Yahweh identifies himself: "I am the LORD your
God, who brought you out of the land of Egypt, out of the
house of bondage" (Deut. 5:6; Ex. 20:2). Yahweh is the one
who frees from bondage. The God of the Bible wants to be
known as the liberator of the oppressed.

The Exodus was certainly the decisive event in the creation
of the chosen people. We distort the biblical interpretation of
this momentous occasion unless we see that at this pivotal
point, the Lord of the universe was at work correcting oppression and liberating the poor.

2. *Destruction and Captivity.* When they settled in the promised land, the Israelites soon discovered that Yahweh's passion
for justice was a two-edged sword. When they were oppressed,
it led to their freedom. But when they became the oppressors,
it led to their destruction.

When God called Israel out of Egypt and made his covenant
with them, he gave them his law so that they could live together in peace and justice. But Israel failed to obey the law of
the covenant. As a result, God destroyed Israel and sent his
chosen people into captivity.

Why?

The explosive message of the prophets is that God destroyed
Israel because of mistreatment of the poor! The Word of the
Lord is this: Economic exploitation sent the chosen people
into captivity.

The middle of the eighth century B.C. was a time of political
success and economic prosperity unknown since the days of
Solomon.[3] But it was precisely at this moment that God sent
his prophet Amos to announce the unwelcome news that the
northern kingdom of Israel would be destroyed. Penetrating
beneath the façade of current prosperity and fantastic eco-

nomic growth, Amos saw terrible oppression of the poor. He saw the rich "trample the head of the poor into the dust of the earth" (2:7). He saw that the affluent lifestyle of the rich was built on oppression of the poor (6:1–7). He denounced the rich women ("cows" was Amos's word!) "who oppress the poor, who crush the needy, who say to their husbands, 'Bring, that we may drink'" (4:1). Even in the courts the poor had no hope because the rich bribed the judges (5:10–15).

Archaeologists have confirmed Amos's picture of shocking extremes of wealth and poverty.[4] In the early days of settlement in Canaan, the land was distributed equally among the families and tribes. All Israelites enjoyed a similar standard of living. In fact as late as the tenth century B.C., archaeologists have found that houses were all approximately the same size. But by Amos's day two centuries later, everything is different. Archaeologists have uncovered bigger, better built houses in one area and poorer houses huddled together in another section.[5] No wonder Amos warned the rich: "You have built houses of hewn stone, but you shall not dwell in them" (5:11).

God's Word through Amos was that the northern kingdom would be destroyed and the people taken into exile (7:11, 17).

> *Woe to those who lie upon beds of ivory,*
> *and stretch themselves upon their couches,*
> *and eat lambs from the flock,*
> *and calves from the midst of the stall . . .*
> *Therefore they shall now be the first of those*
> *to go into exile,*
> *and the revelry of those who stretch themselves*
> *shall pass away. (6:4, 7)*

Only a very few years after Amos spoke, it happened just as God had said. The Assyrians conquered the northern kingdom and took thousands into captivity. Because of their mistreatment of the poor, God destroyed the northern kingdom—forever.

As in the case of the Exodus, we must not ignore other very important factors. The prophet Hosea (a contemporary of Amos) disclosed that the nation's idolatry was another cause of impending destruction. Because they had forsaken Yahweh for idols, the nation would be destroyed (Hos. 8:1–6; 9:1–3).[6]

According to the prophets, then, the northern kingdom fell because of both idolatry and economic exploitation of the poor.

God sent other prophets to announce the same fate for the southern kingdom of Judah. Isaiah warned that destruction from afar would befall Judah because of her mistreatment of the poor:

> *Woe to those who decree iniquitous decrees . . .*
> *to turn aside the needy from justice*
> *and to rob the poor of my people of their right. . .*
> *What will you do on the day of punishment,*
> *in the storm which will come from afar? (Is. 10:1-4)*

Micah denounced those in Judah who "covet fields, and seize them; and houses, and take them away; they oppress a man and his house, a man and his inheritance" (2:2). As a result, he warned, Jerusalem would one day become a "heap of ruins" (3:12).

Fortunately Judah was more open to the prophetic word and the nation was spared for a time. But oppression of the poor continued. A hundred years after the time of Isaiah, the prophet Jeremiah again condemned the wealthy who had amassed riches by oppressing the poor:

> *Wicked men are found among my people;*
> *they lurk like fowlers lying in wait.*
> *They set a trap;*
> *they catch men.*
> *Like a basket full of birds,*
> *their houses are full of treachery;*
> *therefore they have become great and rich,*
> *they have grown fat and sleek.*
> *They know no bounds in deeds of wickedness;*
> *they judge not with justice*
> *the cause of the fatherless, to make it prosper,*
> *and they do not defend the rights of the needy.*
> *Shall I not punish them for these things*
> *says the LORD,*
> *and shall I not avenge myself*
> *on a nation such as this? (Jer. 5:26-29)*

Even at that late date Jeremiah could promise hope if the people would forsake *both* injustice *and* idolatry.

If you truly execute justice one with another, if you do not oppress

the alien, the fatherless or the widow . . . and if you do not go after
other gods to your own hurt, then I will let you dwell in this place,
in the land that I gave of old to your fathers for ever. (Jer. 7:5–7)
But they continued to oppress the poor and helpless (Jer.
34:3–17). As a result Jeremiah persisted in saying God would
use the Babylonians to destroy Judah. In 587 B.C. Jerusalem
fell and the Babylonian captivity began.

The destruction of Israel and Judah, however, was not mere
punishment. God wanted to use the Assyrians and Babylonians
to purge his people of oppression and injustice. In a remarkable
passage Isaiah showed how God would attack his foes and
enemies (that is, his chosen people!) in order to purify them
and restore justice.

> *How the faithful city [Jerusalem]*
>   *has become a harlot,*
>   *she that was full of justice!*
> *Righteousness lodged in her,*
>   *but now murderers.*
> *Your silver has become dross,*
>   *your wine mixed with water. . .*
> *Every one loves a bribe*
> *and runs after gifts.*
> *They do not defend the fatherless,*
> *and the widow's cause does not come to them.*
> *Therefore the Lord says,*
>   *the LORD of hosts,*
>   *the Mighty One of Israel:*
> *"Ah, I will vent my wrath on my enemies,*
>   *and avenge myself on my foes.*
> *I will turn my hand against you*
>   *and will smelt away your dross as with lye*
>   *and remove all your alloy.*
> *And I will restore your judges as at the first,*
>   *and your counsellors as at the beginning.*
> *Afterward you shall be called the city of righteousness,*
>   *the faithful city." (Is. 1:21–26)*

The catastrophe of national destruction and captivity reveals
the God of the Exodus still at work correcting the oppression
of the poor.

3. *The Incarnation.* Christians believe that God revealed himself most completely in Jesus of Nazareth. How did the Incarnate One define his mission?

His words in the synagogue at Nazareth, spoken near the beginning of his public ministry, still throb with hope for the poor. He read from the prophet Isaiah:

The Spirit of the Lord is upon me,
because he has anointed me to preach good news to the poor.
He has sent me to proclaim release to the captives
and recovering of sight to the blind,
to set at liberty those who are oppressed,
to proclaim the acceptable year of the Lord. (Lk. 4:18–19)

After reading these words he informed the audience that this Scripture was now fulfilled in himself. The mission of the Incarnate One was to free the oppressed and heal the blind. (It was also to preach the gospel. And this is *equally* important although the focus of this book precludes further discussion of it.[7]) The poor are the only group specifically singled out as recipients of Jesus' gospel. Certainly the gospel he proclaimed was for all, but he was particularly concerned that the poor realize that his good news was for them.

Some try to avoid the clear meaning of Jesus' statement by spiritualizing his words. Certainly, as other texts show, he came to open our blinded hearts, to die for our sins and to free us from the oppression of guilt. But that is not what he means here. The words about releasing captives and liberating the oppressed are from Isaiah. In their original Old Testament setting, they unquestionably referred to physical oppression and captivity.

Jesus' actual ministry corresponded precisely to the words of Luke 4. He spent most of his time not among the rich and powerful in Jerusalem, but among the poor in the cultural and economic backwater of Galilee. He healed the sick and blind. He fed the hungry. And he warned his followers in the strongest possible words that those who do not feed the hungry, clothe the naked and visit the prisoners will experience eternal damnation (Mt. 25:31–46).

At the supreme moment of history when God took on human flesh, the God of Israel was still liberating the poor and oppressed and summoning his people to do the same. That is the central reason for Christian concern for the poor.

It is not just at the Exodus, captivity and Incarnation, however, that we learn of God's concern for the poor. The Bible is full of passages which speak of this. Two illustrations from the Psalms are typical of a host of other texts.

Psalm 10 begins with despair. God seems to have hidden himself far away while the wicked prosper by oppressing the poor (vv. 2, 9). But the psalmist concludes with hope:

The hapless commits himself to thee;
  thou hast been the helper of the fatherless...
O LORD, thou wilt hear the desire of the meek...
  thou wilt incline thy ear
to do justice to the fatherless and the oppressed. (vv. 14, 17, 18)

Psalm 146 is a ringing declaration that to care for the poor is central to the very nature of God. The psalmist exults in the God of Jacob because he is both the creator of the universe and the defender of the oppressed.

> *Praise the LORD!*
> *Praise the LORD, O my soul!...*
> *Happy is he whose help is the God of Jacob,*
>   *whose hope is in the LORD his God,*
> *who made heaven and earth,*
>   *the sea, and all that is in them;*
> *who keeps faith forever;*
>   *who executes justice for the oppressed;*
>   *who gives food to the hungry.*
> *The LORD sets the prisoners free;*
> *the LORD opens the eyes of the blind.*
> *The LORD lifts up those who are bowed down;*
>   *the LORD loves the righteous.*
> *The LORD watches over the sojourners,*
>   *he upholds the widow and the fatherless;*
>   *but the way of the wicked he brings to ruin.*

According to Scripture it is just as much a part of God's essence to defend the weak, the stranger and the oppressed as to create the universe. Because of who he is,[8] Yahweh lifts up the mistreated. The foundation of Christian concern for the hungry and oppressed is that God cares especially for them.

GOD IDENTIFIES WITH THE POOR God not only acts in history to liberate the poor, but in a mysterious way that we can only half fathom, the Sovereign of the universe identifies with the weak and destitute. Two proverbs state this beautiful truth. Proverbs 14:31 puts it negatively: "He who oppresses a poor man insults his Maker." Even more moving is the positive formulation: "He who is kind to the poor lends to the LORD" (19:17). What a statement! Helping a poor person is like helping the Creator of all things with a loan.

Only in the Incarnation can we begin dimly to perceive what God's identification with the weak, oppressed and poor really means. "Though he was rich," St. Paul says of our Lord Jesus, "yet for your sake he became poor" (2 Cor. 8:9).

He was born in a small, insignificant province of the Roman Empire. His first visitors, the shepherds, were persons viewed as thieves by Jewish society. His parents were too poor to bring the normal offering for purification. Instead of a lamb, they brought two pigeons to the temple.[9] Jesus was a refugee (Mt. 2:13–15) and then an immigrant in Galilee (Mt. 2:19–23). Since Jewish rabbis received no fees for their teaching, Jesus had no regular income during his public ministry. (Scholars belonged to the poorer classes in Judaism.)[10] Nor did he have a home of his own. He warned an eager follower who promised to follow him everywhere, "Foxes have holes, and birds of the air have nests; but the Son of man has nowhere to lay his head" (Mt. 8:20). Jesus also sent out his disciples in extreme poverty (Lk. 9:3; 10:4).

His identification with the poor and unfortunate was, he said, a sign that he was the Messiah. When John the Baptist sent messengers to ask Jesus if he were the long-expected Messiah, Jesus simply pointed to his deeds. He was healing the sick and preaching to the poor (Mt. 11:2–6). Jesus also preached to the rich. But apparently it was his particular concern to preach to the poor that validated his claim to Messiahship. His preoccupation with the poor and disadvantaged contrasted sharply with the style of his contemporaries. Was that perhaps why he added a final word to take back to John: "Blessed is he who takes no offence at me" (Mt. 11:6)?

Only as we feel the presence of the incarnate God in the

form of a poor Galilean can we begin to understand his words:
*I was hungry and you gave me food, I was thirsty and you gave
me drink. . . I was naked and you clothed me . . . Truly, I say to
you, as you did it to one of the least of these my brethren, you did
it to me. (Mt. 25:35–40)*
What does it mean to feed and clothe the Creator of all things?
We cannot know. We can only look on the poor and oppressed
with new eyes and resolve to heal their hurts and help end
their oppression.

If Jesus' saying in Matthew 25:40 is awesome, its parallel is
terrifying. "Truly, I say to you, as you did it not to one of the
least of these, you did it not to me" (v. 45). What does that
mean in a world where millions die each year while rich
Christians live in affluence? What does it mean to see the Lord
of the universe lying by the road side starving and walk by on
the other side? We cannot know. We can only pledge, in fear
and trembling, not to kill him again.

GOD'S SPECIAL INSTRUMENTS When God selected
a chosen people, he picked poor slaves in Egypt. When God
called the early church, most of the members were poor folk.
When God became flesh, he came as a poor Galilean. Are these
facts isolated phenomena or part of a significant pattern? This
is our third question in discerning God's special concern for
the poor.

God might have selected a rich, powerful nation as his chosen
people. Instead he chose oppressed slaves. God picked an
impoverished, enslaved people to be his special instrument of
revelation and salvation for all people. (See also Gideon in
Judges 6:15–16; 7:2.)

In the early church most members were poor. In a recent
book sketching the social history of early Christianity, Martin
Hengel points out that the early Gentile Christian communities "were predominantly poor."[11] St. Paul marvelled at the
kind of people God called into the church:
*Not many of you were wise according to worldly standards, not
many were powerful, not many were of noble birth; but God chose
what is foolish in the world to shame the wise, God chose what is
weak in the world to shame the strong. God chose what is low and*

despised in the world, even things that are not, to bring to nothing things that are, so that no human being might boast in the presence of God. (I Cor. I :26–29)

Likewise James:

My brethren, show no partiality as you hold the faith of our Lord Jesus Christ, the Lord of glory. For if a man with gold rings and in fine clothing comes into your assembly, and a poor man in shabby clothing also comes in, and you pay attention to the one who wears the fine clothing and say, "Have a seat here, please," while you say to the poor man, "Stand there," or, "Sit at my feet," have you not made distinctions among yourselves, and become judges with evil thoughts? Listen, my beloved brethren. Has not God chosen those who are poor in the world to be rich in faith and heirs of the kingdom which he has promised to those who love him? But you have dishonoured the poor man. Is it not the rich who oppress you, is it not they who drag you into court? Is it not they who blaspheme the honourable name which was invoked over you? (Jas. 2 :1–7)

The rhetorical question in verse five indicates that the Jerusalem church too was far from rich. But the entire passage illustrates the way the church so often forsakes God's way and opts instead for the way of the world. At both the Exodus and the emergence of the early church, God chose poor folk as his special instruments.

Of course one must not overstate the case. Abraham seems to have been well off. Moses lived at Pharaoh's court for forty years. Paul and Luke were neither poor nor uneducated. God did not work exclusively through impoverished, oppressed people. There is a sharp contrast, nonetheless, between God's procedure and ours. When we want to effect change, we almost always contact people with influence, prestige and power. When God wanted to save the world, he selected slaves, prostitutes and sundry other disadvantaged folk.

Again we return to the Incarnation. Nowhere is the contrast between God's ways and ours clearer than here. God might have entered history as a powerful Roman emperor or at least as an influential Sadducee with a prominent place in the Sanhedrin. Instead he came and lived as a poor carpenter in the humble hamlet of Nazareth too insignificant to be mentioned either in the Old Testament or the writings of Josephus, the first-century Jewish historian.[12] Yet this is how God chose to effect our salvation.

When Jesus chose his disciples, the persons who were to carry on his mission, all except Matthew were fishermen and other common folk. Those who think that only the rich and powerful change history continue to take offence at Jesus' pre-occupation with the poor and weak.

Again we must oppose the view that God never uses rich, powerful people as his chosen instruments. He has and does. But we *always* choose such people. God, on the other hand, frequently selects the poor to carry out his most important tasks. He sees potential there that we do not. And when the task is done, the poor and weak are less likely to boast that they deserve the credit. God's selection of the lowly to be his special messengers of salvation to the world is striking evidence of his special concern for them. And his Incarnation as a poor Galilean suggests that the frequent use of the poor as his special instruments is not insignificant historical trivia. It points to something significant about the very nature of God.

IS GOD A MARXIST?   Jesus' story of the rich man and Lazarus echoes and illustrates a fourth teaching prominent throughout Scripture: The rich may prosper for a time but eventually God will destroy them; the poor on the other hand, God will exalt.

Mary's Magnificat puts it simply and bluntly:

> *My soul magnifies the Lord. . . .*
> *He has put down the mighty from their thrones,*
>   *and exalted those of low degree ;*
> *he has filled the hungry with good things,*
>   *and the rich he has sent empty away. (Lk. 1 :46–53)*

Centuries earlier Hannah's song had proclaimed the same truth:

> *There is none holy like the LORD,*
>   *there is none besides thee. . . .*
> *Talk no more so very proudly,*
>   *let not arrogance come from your mouth. . . .*
> *The bows of the mighty are broken,*

> but the feeble gird on strength.
> Those who were full have hired themselves out for bread,
>   but those who were hungry have ceased to hunger. . . .
> The LORD makes poor and makes rich. . . .
> He raises up the poor from the dust;
>   he lifts the needy from the ash heap. (1 Sam. 2:2–8)

Jesus pronounced a blessing on the poor and a curse on the rich:

> Blessed are you poor, for yours is
>   the kingdom of God.
> Blessed are you that hunger now, for
>   you shall be satisfied. . . .
> Woe to you that are rich, for you
> have received your consolation.
> Woe to you that are full now, for
>   you shall hunger. (Lk. 6:20–25)[13]

"Come now, you rich, weep and howl for the miseries that are coming upon you" (Jas. 5:1) is a constant theme of biblical revelation.

Why does Scripture declare that God regularly reverses the good fortunes of the rich? Is God engaged in class warfare? Actually our texts never say that God loves the poor more than the rich. But they do constantly assert that God lifts up the poor and disadvantaged. They persistently insist that God casts down the wealthy and powerful—precisely because they became wealthy by oppressing the poor or because they failed to feed the hungry.

Why did James warn the rich to weep and howl because of impending misery? Because they had cheated their workers:

You have laid up treasure for the last days. Behold, the wages of the labourers who mowed your fields, which you kept back by fraud, cry out; and the cries of the harvesters have reached the ears of the Lord of hosts. You have lived on the earth in luxury and in pleasure; you have fattened your hearts in a day of slaughter. (Jas. 5:3–5)

God does not have class enemies. But he hates and punishes injustice and neglect of the poor. And the rich, if we accept the repeated warnings of Scripture, are frequently guilty of both.[14]

Long before the days of James, the psalmist knew that the rich were often rich because of oppression. But he took comfort in the faith that God would punish such evildoers.

In arrogance the wicked hotly pursue the poor....
His ways prosper at all times....
He thinks in his heart, "I shall not be moved;
  throughout all generations I shall not meet adversity...."
  he lurks in secret like a lion in his covert;
he lurks that he may seize the poor,
  he seizes the poor when he draws him into his net....
Arise, O LORD; O God, lift up thy hand;
  forget not the afflicted....
Break thou the arm of the wicked and evildoer....
O LORD, thou wilt hear the desire of the meek;
  thou wilt strengthen their heart,
  thou wilt incline thine ear
to do justice to the fatherless and the oppressed.... (Ps. 10)

God announced the same message through the prophet Jeremiah:

> *Wicked men are found among my people;*
>   *they lurk like fowlers lying in wait.*
> *They set a trap;*
>   *they catch men.*
> *Like a basket full of birds*
>   *their houses are full of treachery;*
> therefore they have become great and rich,
>   they have grown fat and sleek.
> *They know no bounds in deeds of wickedness;*
>   *they judge not with justice*
> *the cause of the fatherless, to make it prosper,*
>   *and they do not defend the rights of the needy.*
> *Shall I not punish them for these things?*
>   *says the LORD. (Jer. 5:26–29, my emphasis)*

Nor was the faith of Jeremiah and the psalmist mere wishful thinking. Through the prophets God announced devastation and destruction for both rich individuals and rich nations who oppressed the poor. And it happened as they predicted. Jeremiah pronounced one of the most biting, satirical diatribes in all of Scripture against the unjust King Jehoiakim of Judah:

"Woe to him who builds his house by unrighteousness,
and his upper rooms by injustice;
who makes his neighbour serve him for nothing,
and does not give him his wages;
who says, 'I will build myself a great house
with spacious upper rooms,'
and cuts out windows for it,
panelling it with cedar,
and painting it with vermillion.
Do you think you are a king
because you compete in cedar?
Did not your father eat and drink
and do justice and righteousness?
Then it was well with him.
He judged the cause of the poor and needy;
then it was well.
Is not this to know me?
But you have eyes and heart
only for your dishonest gain,
for shedding innocent blood,
and for practicing oppression and violence.". . .
Therefore thus says the Lord concerning Jehoiakim. . .
"With the burial of an ass he shall be buried,
dragged and cast forth beyond the gates of Jerusalem."
(Jer. 22:13–19)

Jehoiakim, historians think, was assassinated.[15]

God destroys whole nations as well as rich individuals because of oppression of the poor. We have already examined a
few of the pertinent texts at the beginning of this chapter.[16]
One more is important. Through Isaiah God declared that the
rulers of Judah were rich because they had cheated the poor.
Surfeited with affluence, the wealthy women had indulged in
self-centred wantonness, oblivious to the suffering of the
oppressed. The result, God said, would be destruction.

The Lord enters into judgement
with the elders and princes of his people:
"It is you who have devoured the vineyard,
the spoil of the poor is in your houses.
What do you mean by crushing my people,

> *by grinding the face of the poor?"*
> > *says the LORD GOD of hosts.*
> *The Lord said:*
> *Because the daughters of Zion are haughty*
> > *and walk with outstretched necks;*
> > *glancing wantonly with their eyes,*
> *mincing along as they go,*
> > *tinkling with their feet;*
> > *the Lord will smite with a scab*
> > *the heads of the daughters of Zion. . . .*
> *In that day the Lord will take away the finery*
> > *of the anklets, the headbands, and the crescents. . . .*
> *Instead of perfume there will be rottenness;*
> > *and instead of a girdle, a rope;*
> *and instead of well-set hair, baldness;*
> > *and instead of a rich robe, a girding of sackcloth;*
> > *instead of beauty, shame.*
> *Your men shall fall by the sword*
> > *and your mighty men in battle. (Is. 3:14-25, my emphasis)*

Because the rich oppress the poor and weak, the Lord of history is at work pulling down their houses and kingdoms.

Sometimes Scripture does not charge the rich with direct oppression of the poor. It simply accuses them of failure to share with the needy. But the result is the same.

In the story of the rich man and Lazarus (Lk. 16), Jesus does not say that the rich man exploited Lazarus. He merely shows that he had no concern for the sick beggar lying outside his gate. "Clothed in purple and fine linen," the rich man "feasted sumptuously every day" (Lk. 16:19). Lazarus on the other hand, "desired to be fed with what fell from the rich man's table" (Lk. 16:21). Did the rich man deny hungry Lazarus even the scraps? Perhaps not. But obviously he had no real concern for him. Such sinful neglect of the needy infuriates the God of the poor. When Lazarus died, God comforted him in Abraham's bosom. When the rich man died, torment confronted him.[17] The meaning of the name Lazarus, "one whom God has helped,"[18] underlines the basic point. God aids the poor, but the rich he sends empty away.

Clark Pinnock, of Regent College, is surely correct when he

notes that "a story like that of Dives and Lazarus ought to explode in our hands when we read it sitting at our well-covered tables while the third world stands outside."[19] Not only the law and the prophets but our Lord himself declares the terrifying word that God destroys the rich when they fail to assist the poor.

The biblical explanation of Sodom's destruction provides another illustration of this terrible truth. If asked why Sodom was destroyed, virtually all Christians would point to the city's gross sexual perversity. But that is a one-sided recollection of what Scripture actually teaches. Ezekiel shows that one important reason God destroyed Sodom was that she stubbornly refused to share with the poor!

Behold, this was the guilt of your sister Sodom: she and her daughters had pride, surfeit of food, and prosperous ease, but did not aid the poor and needy. *They were haughty, and did abominable things before me; therefore I removed them, when I saw it.* (Ezek. 16:49–50, my emphasis)[20]

The text does not say that they oppressed the poor (although they probably did). It simply accuses them of failing to assist the needy.

Affluent Christians remember Sodom's sexual misconduct and forget her sinful unconcern for the poor. Is it because the former is less upsetting? Have we allowed our economic self-interest to distort our interpretation of Scripture? Undoubtedly we have. But precisely to the extent that our affirmation of scriptural authority is sincere, we will permit painful texts to correct our thinking. As we do, we will acknowledge in fear and trembling that the God of the Bible wreaks horrendous havoc on the rich. But it is not because he does not love rich persons. It is because the rich regularly oppress the poor and neglect the needy.

GOD'S CONCERN AND OURS   Since God cares so much for the poor, it is hardly surprising that he wants his people to do the same. God's command to believers to have a special regard for the poor, weak and disadvantaged is the fifth theme of biblical literature we shall follow.

Equal justice for the poor in court is a constant theme of

Scripture. The law commanded it (Ex. 23:6). The psalmist invoked divine assistance for the king so that he could provide it (Ps. 72:1-4). And the prophets announced destruction because the rulers stubbornly subverted it (Amos 5:10-15).

Widows, orphans and strangers also receive particularly frequent attention.

You shall not wrong a stranger or oppress him, for you were strangers in the land of Egypt. You shall not afflict any widow or orphan. If you do afflict them, and they cry out to me, I will surely hear their cry; and my wrath will burn, and I will kill you with the sword, and your wives shall become widows and your children fatherless. (Ex. 22:21-24)

"The fatherless, widows, and foreigners," John F. Alexander observes, "each have about forty verses that command justice for them. God wants to make it very clear that in a special sense he is the protector of these weak ones. Strangers are to be treated nearly the same as Jews, and woe to people who take advantage of orphans or widows."[21]

Rare indeed are the Christians who pay any attention to Jesus' command to show "bias" toward the poor in their dinner invitations.

When you give a dinner or a banquet, do not invite your friends or your brothers or your kinsmen or rich neighbours. . . . But when you give a feast, invite the poor, the maimed, the lame, the blind, and you will be blessed because they cannot repay you. (Lk. 14: 12-14)[22]

Obviously Jesus was employing hyperbole, a typical technique of Hebrew literature to emphasize his point. He did not mean to forbid parties with friends and relatives. But he certainly did mean that we ought to entertain the poor and disadvantaged (who cannot reciprocate) at least as often—and perhaps a lot more often—than we entertain friends, relatives and "successful" folk. Have you ever known a Christian who took Jesus that seriously?

The Bible specifically commands believers to imitate God's special concern for the poor and oppressed. In the Old Testament, Yahweh frequently reminded the Israelites of their former oppression in Egypt when he commanded them to care for the poor. God's unmerited concern for the Hebrew slaves in Egyptian bondage is the model to imitate (Ex. 22:21–24; Deut. 15:13–15).

Jesus taught his followers to imitate God's mercy in their lending as well!

If you do good to those who do good to you, what credit is that to you? . . . And if you lend to those from whom you hope to receive, what credit is that to you? . . . Lend, expecting nothing in return; and your reward will be great, and you will be sons of the Most High; for he is kind to the ungrateful and the selfish. Be merciful, even as your Father is merciful. (Lk. 6:33–36)

Why lend without expecting return? Because that is the way our Father acts. Jesus' followers are to reverse normal human patterns precisely because they are sons of God and want to reflect his nature.

When Paul took up the collection for the poor in Jerusalem, he pointedly reminded the Corinthians that the Lord Jesus became poor so that they might become rich (2 Cor. 8:9). When the author of 1 John called on Christians to share with the needy, he first mentioned the example of Christ: "By this we know love, that he laid down his life for us; and we ought to lay down our lives for the brethren" (1 Jn. 3:16). Then, in the very next verse, he urged Christians to give generously to the needy. It is the amazing self-sacrifice of Christ which Christians are to imitate as they relate to the poor and oppressed.

We have seen that God's Word commands believers to care for the poor. In fact the Bible underlines the command by teaching that when God's people care for the poor, they imitate God himself. But that is not all. God's Word teaches that those who neglect the poor and oppressed are really not God's people at all—no matter how frequent their religious rituals or how orthodox their creeds and confessions.

God thundered again and again through the prophets that worship in the context of mistreatment of the poor and disadvantaged is an outrage. Isaiah denounced Israel (he called her Sodom and Gomorrah!) because she tried to worship Yahweh and oppress the weak at the same time:

> *Hear the word of the LORD,*
> *you rulers of Sodom!*

> Give ear to the teaching of our God,
>   you people of Gomorrah!
> What to me is the multitude of your sacrifices? . . .
> Bring no more vain offerings;
>   incense is an abomination to me.
> New moon and sabbath and the calling of assemblies—
>   I cannot endure iniquity and solemn assembly.
> Your new moons and your appointed feasts
>   my soul hates; . . .
> even though you make many prayers,
>   I will not listen;
>   your hands are full of blood. (Is. 1:10–15)

What does God want? "Cease to do evil, learn to do good; seek justice, correct oppression; defend the fatherless, plead for the widow" (Is. 1:16–17).

Equally powerful are Isaiah's words against mixing fasting and injustice:

> 'Why have we fasted, and thou seest it not?
> Why have we humbled ourselves,
> and thou takest no knowledge of it?'
> Behold, in the day of your fast you seek your own pleasure,
>   and oppress all your workers. . .
> Is not this the fast that I choose:
>   to loose the bonds of wickedness,
>   to undo the thongs of the yoke,
> to let the oppressed go free,
>   and to break every yoke?
> Is it not to share your bread with the hungry,
>   and bring the homeless poor into your house? (Is. 58:3–7)

God's words through the prophet Amos are also harsh:

> I hate, I despise your feasts,
>   and I take no delight in your solemn assemblies.
> Even though you offer me your burnt offerings
>   and cereal offerings,
>   I will not accept them. . .
> But let justice roll down like waters,
>   and righteousness like an overflowing stream.
> (Amos 5:21–24)[23]

Earlier in Amos 5 the prophet had condemned the rich and

powerful for oppressing the poor. They even bribed judges to prevent redress in the courts. God wants justice, not religious rituals, from such people.[24] Their worship is a mockery and abomination to the God of the poor.

Nor has God changed. Jesus repeated the same theme. He warned the people about the scribes "who devour widows' houses and for a pretence make long prayers" (Mk. 12:38–40). Their pious-looking garments and frequent visits to the synagogue were a sham. Jesus was a Hebrew prophet in the tradition of Amos and Isaiah. Like them, he announced God's outrage against those who try to mix pious practices and mistreatment of the poor.

The prophetic word against religious hypocrites raises an extremely difficult question. Are the people of God truly God's people if they oppress the poor? Is the church really the church if it does not work to free the oppressed?

We have seen how God declared that the people of Israel were really Sodom and Gomorrah rather than the people of God (Is. 1:10). God simply could not tolerate their exploitation of the poor and disadvantaged any longer. Hosea solemnly announced that because of their sins, Israel was no longer God's people and he was no longer their God (Hos. 1:8–9). In fact God destroyed them. Jesus was even more blunt and sharp. To those who do not feed the hungry, clothe the naked and visit the prisoners, he will speak a terrifying word at the final judgement: "Depart from me, you cursed, into the eternal fire prepared for the devil and his angels" (Mt. 25:41). The meaning is clear and unambiguous. Jesus intends that his disciples imitate his own special concern for the poor and needy. Those who disobey will experience eternal damnation.

But perhaps we have misinterpreted Matt. 25. Some people think that "the least of these" (v. 45) and "the least of these my brethren" (v. 40) refer only to Christians. This exegesis is not certain. But even if the primary reference of these words is to poor believers, other aspects of Jesus' teaching not only permit but *require* us to extend the meaning of Matt. 25 to both believers and unbelievers who are poor and oppressed. The story of the good Samaritan (Lk. 10:29ff) teaches that anybody in need is our neighbour. Matt. 5:43ff is even more explicit:

You have heard that it was said, "You shall love your neighbour and hate your enemy." But I say to you, love your enemies and pray for those who persecute you, so that you may be sons of your Father who is in heaven; for he makes his sun rise on the evil and on the good, and sends rain on the just and on the unjust.

The ideal in the Qumran community (known to us through the Dead Sea Scrolls) was indeed to "Love all the sons of light" and "hate all the sons of darkness" (I QS 1:9–10). Even in the Old Testament, Israelites were commanded to love the neighbour who was the son of their own people and ordered not to seek the prosperity of Ammonites and Moabites (Lev. 19:17–18; Deut. 23:3–6). But Jesus explicitly forbids his followers to limit their loving concern to the neighbour who is a member of their own ethnic or religious group. He explicitly commands his followers to imitate God who does good for all people everywhere.

As George Ladd has said, "Jesus redefines the meaning of love for neighbour; it means love for any man in need."[25] In light of the parable of the Good Samaritan and the clear teaching of Matt. 5:43ff, one is compelled to say that part of the full teaching of Matt. 25 is that those who fail to aid the poor and oppressed (whether they are believers or not) are simply not the people of God.

Lest we forget the warning, God repeats it in 1 John 3:17–18. "But if any one has the world's goods and sees his brother in need, yet closes his heart against him, how does God's love abide in him? Little children, let us not love in word or speech but in deed and in truth." (See also, James 2:14–17.) Again the words are plain. What do they mean for Western Christians who demand increasing affluence each year while Christians in the Third World suffer malnutrition, deformed bodies and brains—even starvation? The text clearly says that if we fail to aid the needy, we do not have God's love—no matter what we may say. It is deeds that count, not pious phrases and saintly speeches. Regardless of what we do or say at 11:00 a.m. Sunday morning, affluent people who neglect the poor are not the people of God.

But still the question persists. Are professing believers no longer Christians because of continuing sin? Obviously not.

The Christian knows that sinful selfishness continues to plague even the most saintly. We are members of the people of God not because of our own righteousness but solely because of Christ's death for us.

But that response is inadequate. Matthew 25 and 1 John 3 surely mean more than that the people of God are disobedient (but still justified all the same) when they neglect the poor. These verses pointedly assert that some people so disobey God that they are not his people at all in spite of their pious profession. Neglect of the poor is one of the oft-repeated biblical signs of such disobedience. Certainly none of us would claim that we fulfil Matthew 25 perfectly. And we cling to the hope of forgiveness. But there comes a point (and, thank God, he alone knows where!) when neglect of the poor is no longer forgiven. It is punished. Eternally.

Is it not possible—indeed very probable—that a vast majority of Western "Christians" have reached that point? North Americans earn fourteen times as much as the people in India, but they give a very small amount to the church. Most churches spend much of that pitiful pittance on themselves. Can we claim that we are obeying the biblical command to have a special concern for the poor? Can we honestly say that we are imitating God's concern for the poor and oppressed? Can we seriously hope to experience eternal love rather than eternal separation from the God of the poor?

The biblical teaching that Yahweh has a special concern for the poor and oppressed is unambiguous. But does that mean, as some assert today, that God is biased in favour of the poor? Not really. Scripture explicitly forbids being partial. "You shall do no injustice in judgement; you shall not be partial to the poor or defer to the great, but in righteousness shall you judge your neighbour" (Lev. 19:15; also Deut. 1:17). Exodus 23:3 contains precisely the same injunction: "Nor shall you be partial to a poor man in his suit." God instructs his people to be impartial because he himself is not biased.

The most crucial point for us, however, is not God's impartiality, but rather the result of his freedom from bias. The text declares Yahweh's impartiality and then immediately portrays God's tender care for the weak and disadvantaged.

For the LORD your God is God of gods and LORD of lords, the great, the mighty, and the terrible God, who is not partial and takes no bribe. He executes justice for the fatherless and the widow, and loves the sojourner, giving him food and clothing. (Deut. 10:17–18, my emphasis)

God is not partial. He has the same loving concern for each person he has created.[26] Precisely for that reason he cares as much for the weak and disadvantaged as he does for the strong and fortunate. By contrast with the way you and I, as well as the comfortable and powerful of every age and society, always act toward the poor, God seems to have an overwhelming bias in favour of the poor. But he is biased only in contrast with our sinful unconcern. It is only when we take our perverse preference for the successful and wealthy as natural and normative that God's concern appears biased.

God, however, is not neutral. His freedom from bias does not mean that he maintains neutrality in the struggle for justice. God is on the side of the poor! The Bible clearly and repeatedly teaches that God is at work in history casting down the rich and exalting the poor because frequently the rich are wealthy precisely because they have oppressed the poor or have neglected to aid the needy. As we shall see in the next chapter, God also sides with the poor because he disapproves of extremes of wealth and poverty. The God of the Bible is on the side of the poor just because he is *not* biased, for he is a God of impartial justice.

The rich neglect or oppose justice because justice demands that they end their oppression and share with the poor. Therefore God actively opposes the rich. But that does not in any way mean that he loves the rich less than the poor. God longs for the salvation of the rich as much as for the salvation of the poor. He desires fulfilment, joy and happiness for all his creatures. But that does not contradict the fact that he is on the side of the poor. Genuine biblical repentance and conversion lead people to turn away from all sin—including economic oppression.[27] Salvation for the rich will include liberation from their injustice. Thus God's desire for the salvation and fulfilment of the rich is in complete harmony with the scriptural teaching that God is on the side of the poor.

God's concern for the poor is astonishing and boundless. At the pivotal points of revelation history, Yahweh was at work liberating the oppressed. We can only begin to fathom the depth of his identification with the poor disclosed in the Incarnation. Frequently the poor are his specially chosen instruments of revelation and salvation. His passion for justice compels him to obliterate rich societies and individuals that oppress the poor and neglect the needy. Consequently, God's people—if they are indeed his people—follow in the footsteps of the God of the poor.

ECONOMIC RELATIONSHIPS AMONG THE PEOPLE OF GOD

I DO NOT MEAN THAT OTHERS SHOULD BE EASED AND YOU BURDENED, BUT THAT AS A MATTER OF EQUALITY YOUR ABUNDANCE AT THE PRESENT TIME SHOULD SUPPLY THEIR WANT, SO THAT THEIR ABUNDANCE MAY SUPPLY YOUR WANT, THAT THERE MAY BE EQUALITY. AS IT IS WRITTEN, "HE WHO GATHERED MUCH HAD NOTHING OVER, AND HE WHO GATHERED LITTLE HAD NO LACK." [2 CORINTHIANS 8:13-15]

God requires radically transformed economic relationships among his people. Sin has alienated us from God and from each other. The result has been personal selfishness, structural injustice and economic oppression. Among the people of God, however, the power of sin is broken. The new community of the redeemed begins to display an entirely new set of personal, social and economic relationships. The present quality of life among the people of God is to be a sign of that coming perfection and justice which will be revealed when the kingdoms of this world finally and completely become the kingdom of our Lord.

In this chapter we will look at some central biblical models of transformed economic relationships. We discover in the Scriptures that God created mechanisms and structures to prevent great economic inequality among his people. As economic relationships are redeemed in the body of Christ, the church's common life of mutual availability is to point convincingly to the coming kingdom. And—as if that were not enough—the loving oneness among Christians is to become so visible and concrete that it convinces the world that Jesus came from the Father (Jn. 17:20–23).

THE JUBILEE PRINCIPLE Leviticus 25 is one of the most radical texts in all of Scripture. At least it seems that way for people born in countries committed to laissez-faire economics. Every fifty years, God said, all land was to return to the original owners—without compensation! Physical handicaps, death of a breadwinner or lack of natural ability may lead some people to become poorer than others. But God does not want such disadvantages to lead to greater and greater divergence of wealth and poverty. God therefore gave his people a law which would equalize land ownership every fifty years (Lev. 25:10–24).

In an agricultural society land is capital. Land was the basic means of producing wealth in Israel. At the beginning, of course, the land had been divided more or less equally among the tribes and families. Apparently God wanted that basic economic equality to continue. Hence his command to return all land to the original owners every fifty years. Private property was not abolished. But the means of producing wealth were to be equalized regularly.

What is the theological basis for this startling command? Yahweh's ownership of everything is the presupposition. The land cannot be sold permanently because Yahweh owns it: "The land shall not be sold in perpetuity, *for the land is mine;* for you are strangers and sojourners with me" (Lev. 25:23, my emphasis). God owns the land! For a time he permits his people to sojourn on his good earth, cultivate it, eat its produce and enjoy its beauty. But we are only stewards.

Before and after the year of Jubilee, land could be bought or sold. But the buyer actually purchased a specific number of harvests, not the land itself (Lev. 25:16). And woe betide the person who tried to make a killing by demanding what the market would bear rather than a just price for the intervening harvests from the date of purchase to the next Jubilee. "If the years are many you shall increase the price, and if the years are few you shall diminish the price, for it is the number of the crops that he is selling to you. You shall not wrong one another, but you shall fear your God; for I am the LORD your God" (Lev. 25:16–17). Yahweh is Lord—even of economics! There is no hint here of some sacred law of supply and demand totally independent of biblical ethics and the lordship of Yahweh. The people of God submit to him, and he demands economic justice among his people.

That this passage prescribes justice rather than haphazard handouts by wealthy philanthropists is extremely significant. The year of Jubilee envisages an institutionalized structure that affects everyone automatically. It is to be the poor person's *right* to receive back his inheritance at the time of Jubilee. Returning the land is not a charitable courtesy that the wealthy may extend if they please.[1]

The Jubilee Principle also provides for self-help and self-development. With his land returned, the poor person could again earn his own living. The biblical concept of Jubilee underlines the importance of institutionalized mechanisms and structures that promote justice.

One final aspect of Leviticus 25 is striking. It is surely more than coincidental that the trumpet blast announcing the Jubilee sounded forth on the day of atonement (Lev. 25:9)! Reconciliation with God is the precondition for reconciliation with brothers and sisters.[2] Conversely, genuine reconciliation with God leads inevitably to a transformation of all other relationships. Reconciled with God by the sacrifice on the day of atonement, the more prosperous Israelites were to liberate the poor by freeing Hebrew slaves as well as returning all land to the original owners.[3]

Unfortunately, we do not know whether the people of Israel ever practiced the year of Jubilee. The absence of references to Jubilee in the historical books suggests that it may never have been implemented.[4] Regardless of its antiquity or implementation, Leviticus 25 remains a part of God's authoritative Word. Because he disapproves of extremes of wealth among his people, God ordains equalizing mechanisms like the year of Jubilee.

THE SABBATICAL YEAR The law also provides for liberation of soil, slaves and debtors every seven years. Again the concern is justice for the poor and disadvantaged.

Every seven years the land is to lie fallow (Ex. 23:10–11; Lev. 25:2–7).[5] The purpose, apparently, is both ecological and humanitarian. Not planting any crops every seventh year certainly helps preserve the fertility of the soil. God, however, is particularly concerned with the poor: "For six years you shall sow your land and gather in its yield; but the seventh year you shall let it rest and lie fallow, *that the poor of your people may eat*" (Ex. 23:10–11, my emphasis). In the seventh year the poor are free to gather for themselves whatever grows by itself in the fields and vineyards.

Hebrew slaves also receive their freedom in the sabbatical year (Deut. 15:12–18). Poverty sometimes forced Israelites to sell themselves as slaves to more prosperous neighbours (Lev. 25:39–40).[6] But this inequality, God decrees, is not to be permanent. At the end of six years the Hebrew slaves are to be set free. And masters are to share the proceeds of their joint labours with the departing brothers: "And when you let him go free from you, you shall not let him go empty-handed; you shall furnish him liberally out of your flock, out of your threshing floor and out of your wine press; as the LORD your God has blessed you, you shall give to him" (Deut. 15:12–14; see also Ex. 21:2–6). The freed slave would thereby have the means to earn his own way.[7]

The sabbatical provision on loans is even more revolutionary (Deut. 15:1–6). Every seven years all debts are to be cancelled! Yahweh even adds a footnote for those with a sharp eye for loopholes: It is sinful to refuse a loan to a poor man just because it is the sixth year and the money will be lost in twelve months.

Take heed lest there be a base thought in your heart, and you say, "The seventh year, the year of release is near," and your eye be hostile to your poor brother, and you give him nothing, and he cry to the LORD against you, and it be sin in you. You shall give to

81

him freely, and your heart shall not be grudging when you give to him; because for this the LORD your God will bless you. (Deut. 15:9–10)[8]

As in the case of the year of Jubilee, it is crucial to note that Scripture prescribes justice rather than mere charity. The sabbatical release of debts was an institutionalized mechanism for preventing an ever-growing gap between rich and poor.

Deuteronomy 15 is both an idealistic statement of God's perfect demand and also a realistic reference to Israel's probable performance concerning debts. Verse 4 promises that there will be no poor in Israel—if they obey all the commands God provides! But God knew they would not attain that standard. Hence the recognition in verse 11 that poor people will always exist in Israel. But the conclusion is not that one can therefore ignore the needy because hordes of paupers will always far exceed one's resources. It is precisely the opposite. "For the poor will never cease out of the land; *therefore* I command you, You shall open wide your hand to your brother, to the needy and to the poor, in the land." (Emphasis added.) Jesus knew (Mt. 26:11) and Deuteronomy implies that sinful persons and societies will always produce poor people. Rather than justifying negligence, however, God intends this insight to lead to renewed concern for the needy and to the creation of structural mechanisms for promoting justice.

The sabbatical year, unfortunately, was practised only sporadically. In fact some texts suggest that failure to obey this law was one reason for the Babylonian exile (2 Chron. 36:20–21; Lev. 26:35–36).[9] Israel's disobedience, however, does not weaken God's demand. Institutionalized structures to reduce poverty and great economic inequality are God's will for his people.

LAWS ON TITHING AND GLEANING Other legal provisions extend the concern of the year of Jubilee and the sabbatical year. The law calls for one-tenth of all farm produce, whether animal, grain or wine, to be set aside as a tithe. "At the end of every three years you shall bring forth all the tithe of your produce in the same year ... and the Levite ... and the sojourner, the fatherless, and the widow, who are within your towns, shall come and eat and be filled; that the LORD your God may bless you" (Deut. 14:28–29; see also Lev. 27:30–32; Deut. 26:12–15; Num. 18:21–32).[10]

The poor widow Ruth was able to survive because of this law of gleaning. When she and Naomi returned to Bethlehem penniless, the grandmother of King David went into the fields at harvest time and gathered the stalks of grain dropped by the gleaners (Ruth 2). She could do that because God's law decreed that farmers should leave some of the harvest, including the corners of grain fields, for the poor. Grapes that had been dropped accidentally were to be left. "You shall leave them for the poor and the sojourner: I am the LORD your God" (Lev. 19:9–10).

The memory of their own poverty and oppression in Egypt was to prompt them to leave generous gleanings for the poor sojourner, the widow and the fatherless. "You shall remember that you were a slave in the land of Egypt; therefore I command you to do this" (Deut. 24:19–22). The law of gleaning was an established method for preventing debilitating poverty among the people of God and sojourners in the land.

MODELS TO FOLLOW AND AVOID How do we apply biblical revelation on the year of Jubilee, the sabbatical year, tithes and gleaning today? Should we attempt to implement these mechanisms? Are these laws, even the basic principles, applicable to the church at all?

God gave Israel the law so that his people would know how to live together in peace and justice. The church is now the new people of God (Gal. 6:16; 3:6–9; 1 Pet. 2:9–10). Certainly, as Paul and other New Testament writers indicate, parts of the Mosaic law (the ceremonial law, for instance) no longer apply to the church. But there is no indication that the moral law has ceased to be normative for Christians (Mt. 5:17–20; Rom. 8: 4).[11] The Old Testament's revelation about the kind of economic relationships that promote love and harmony among God's people should still guide the church today. (Whether these laws have any relevance for society as a whole will be discussed in chapter nine.)

How then do we apply the actual laws we have discussed?

Should we attempt to revive the specific mechanisms proposed in Leviticus 25 and Deuteronomy 15?

Actually, it might not be a bad idea to try the Jubilee itself at least once. It has been somewhat more than fifty years since the people of God divided their capital equally among themselves. We could select 1980 as the Jubilee year in order to give us a little time for preliminary preparations. In 1980 all Christians worldwide would pool all their stocks, bonds, and income producing property and businesses and redistribute them equally. The world would be startled. There would undoubtedly be a certain amount of confusion and disruption. But then good things are seldom easy. Certainly the evangelistic impact of such an act would be fantastic. In a world tragically divided between the haves and have-nots, such a visible demonstration of our oneness in Christ might indeed convince millions that Jesus was from the Father.

Still, I certainly do not think that the specific provisions of the year of Jubilee are binding today. Modern technological society is vastly different from rural Palestine. If Kansas farmers left grain standing in the corners of their fields, it would not help the hungry in inner city New York or rural India. We need methods appropriate to our own civilization. It is the basic principles, not the specific details, which are important and normative for Christians today.

The history of the prohibition against charging interest is instructive at this point. The annual rate of interest in the ancient Near East was incredibly high—often as much as 25 per cent or more.[12] It is not hard, therefore, to see why the law includes prohibitions against charging interest to fellow Israelites (Ex. 22:25; Deut. 23:19-20; Lev. 25:35-38).[13] The *International Critical Commentary* suggests that this legislation reflects a time when most loans were charitable loans rather than commercial ones. Commercial loans to establish or extend a business were not common. Most were charitable loans needed by a poor person or by someone facing a temporary emergency.[14] It is quite clear that the well-being of the poor is a central concern of the texts on interest. "If you lend money to any of my people with you who is poor, you shall not be to him as a creditor, and you shall not exact interest from him" (Ex. 22:25). The legislation on interest is one part of an extensive set of laws designed to protect the poor and prevent great extremes of wealth and poverty among the people of God.

Failing to understand this, the Christian church attempted to apply the texts on interest in a legalistic way. Several church councils wrestled with the question. Eventually, all interest on loans was prohibited in 1179 (Third Lateran Council). But the results were tragic. Medieval monarchs invited Jews (who were not bound by the church's teaching) into their realms to be money lenders. Ghastly anti-Semitism was one demonic result. Increasingly, theologians developed casuistic schemes for circumventing the prohibition.[15] Tragically, the misguided preoccupation with the letter of the law and the resulting adoption of an unworkable, legalistic application helped discredit or at least obscure the important biblical teaching that the God of the poor is Lord of economics—Lord even of interest rates. Legalistic utilization of the texts on interest thus helped create the modern mentality which views loans, banking, indeed the whole field of economics, as completely independent and autonomous. From the standpoint of revealed faith, of course, such a view is heretical. It stems from modern secularism, not the Bible.

This history warns us against a wooden application. But it dare not lead to timid silence. These texts unquestionably teach that the borrowers' need, rather than careful calculation of potential profit, must be decisive for the Christian lender. (Low-interest or no-interest loans for development provided by Christian organizations to Christians in the Third World are an example of meaningful, contemporary application of God's Word on interest.)

In applying the biblical teaching on the year of Jubilee, the sabbatical year, gleaning and tithing then, we must discover the underlying principles. Then we can search for contemporary strategies to give flesh to these basic principles. The texts we have examined clearly show that God wills justice, not mere charity. Therefore Christians should design and institute new structures that can effectively eliminate indigence among believers, and drastically reduce the scandalous extremes of wealth and poverty between rich and poor members of the one body of the risen Jesus.

JESUS' NEW COMMUNITY Let us see how the first-century Christians reaffirmed the Old Testament teaching. Jesus walked the roads of Galilee announcing the startling news that the kingdom of peace and righteousness was at hand. Economic relationships in the new community of his followers were a powerful sign confirming this awesome announcement.

The Hebrew prophets had predicted more than that Israel would be destroyed because of her idolatry and oppression of the poor. They had also proclaimed a message of hope—the hope of a future messianic kingdom. The days are coming, they promised, when God will raise up a righteous Branch from the Davidic line. Peace, righteousness and justice will then abound in a new, redeemed society. When the shoot from the stump of Jesse comes, Isaiah predicted, the poor and meek will finally receive their due: "With righteousness he shall judge the poor, and decide with equity for the meek of the earth" (Is. 11:4; see also Is. 9:6–7; 61:1; Jer. 23:5; Hos. 2:18–20).

The essence of the good news which Jesus proclaimed was that the expected messianic kingdom had come.[16] Certainly the kingdom Jesus announced disappointed popular Jewish expectations. He did not recruit an army to drive out the Romans. He did not attempt to establish a free Jewish state. But neither did he remain alone as an isolated, individualistic prophet. He called and trained disciples. He established a visible community of disciples joined together by their submission to him as Lord. His new community began to live the values of the promised kingdom which was already breaking into the present. As a result, all relationships, even economic ones, were transformed in the community of Jesus' followers.

They shared a common purse (Jn. 12:6).[17] Judas administered the common fund, buying provisions or giving to the poor at Jesus' direction (Jn. 13:29). Nor did this new community of sharing end with Jesus and the Twelve. It included a number of women whom Jesus had healed. The women

86

travelled with Jesus and the disciples, sharing their financial resources with them (Lk. 8:1–3; see also Mk. 15:40–41).[18]

From this perspective, some of Jesus' words gain new meaning and power. Consider his advice to the rich young man.

When Jesus asked the rich young man to sell his goods and give to the poor, he did not say "Become destitute and friendless." Rather, he said, "Come follow me" (Mt. 19:21). In other words, he invited him to join a community of sharing and love, where his security would not be based on individual property holdings, but on openness to the Spirit and on the loving care of new-found brothers and sisters.[19]

Jesus invited the rich young man to share the joyful common life of his new kingdom.

Jesus' words in Mark 10:29–30 have long puzzled me: "Truly, I say to you, there is no one who has left house or brothers or sisters or mother or father or children or lands, for my sake and for the gospel, who will not receive a hundred-fold *now in this time, houses and brothers and sisters and mothers and children and lands,* with persecutions, and in the age to come eternal life" (my emphasis). Matthew 6 contains a similar saying. We are all very—indeed embarrassingly—familiar with the way Jesus urged his followers to enjoy a care-free life unburdened by anxiety over food, clothing and possessions (Mt. 6:25–33). But he ended his advice with a promise too good to be true: "But seek first his kingdom and his righteousness, and all these things [that is, food, clothing, and so on] shall be yours as well." These promises used to seem at least a trifle naive. But his words came alive with meaning when I read them in the context of the new community of Jesus' followers. Jesus began a new social order, a new kingdom of faithful followers who were to be completely available to each other.

The common purse of Jesus' disciples symbolized that unlimited liability for each other. In that new community there would be genuine economic security. Each would indeed have many more loving brothers and sisters than before. The economic resources available in difficult times would in fact be compounded a hundredfold and more. The resources of the entire community of obedient disciples would be available to anyone in need. To be sure, that kind of unselfish, sharing lifestyle would challenge surrounding society so pointedly that there would be persecutions. But even in the most desperate days, the promise would not be empty. Even if persecution led to death, children of martyred parents would receive new mothers and fathers in the community of believers. In the community of the redeemed, all relationships are being transformed. Jesus and his first followers vividly demonstrate that the old covenant's pattern of economic relationships among the people of God is continued and deepened.

THE JERUSALEM MODEL However embarrassing it may be to some, the massive economic sharing of the earliest Christian church is indisputable. "Now the company of those who believed were of one heart and soul, and no one said that any of the things which he possessed was his own, but they had everything in common" (Acts 4:32). Everywhere in the early chapters of Acts, the evidence is abundant and unambiguous (Acts 2:43–47; 4:32–37; 5:1–11; 6:1–7). The early church continued the pattern of economic sharing practised by Jesus.

Economic sharing in the Jerusalem church started in the earliest period. Immediately after reporting the three thousand conversions at Pentecost, Acts notes that "all who believed were together and had all things in common" (2:44). Whenever anyone was in need, they shared. Giving surplus income to needy brothers and sisters was not enough. They regularly dipped into capital reserves, selling property to aid the needy. Barnabas sold a field he owned (4:36, 37). Ananias and Sapphira sold property although they lied about the price. God's promise to Israel (Deut. 15:4)[20] that faithful obedience would eliminate poverty among his people came true! "*There was not a needy person among them,* for as many as were possessors of lands or houses sold them . . . and distribution was made to each as any had need" (Acts 4:34–35).

Two millenia later, the texts still throb with the first community's joy and excitement. They ate meals together "with glad and generous hearts" (Acts 2:46). They experienced an exciting unity as all sensed they "were of one heart and soul"

(Acts 4:32). They were not isolated individuals struggling alone to follow Jesus. A new community in which all areas of life (including economics) were being transformed, became a joyful reality.

The evangelistic impact of their demonstration of oneness is striking. The texts repeatedly relate the transformed economic relationships in the Jerusalem church to the phenomenal evangelistic outreach. "And day by day, attending the temple together and breaking bread in their homes, they partook of food with glad and generous hearts, praising God *and having favour with all the people*. And the Lord added to their number day by day" (Acts 2:46–47, my emphasis). The joy and love exhibited in their common life was contagious! I mentioned before that the author records in Acts 4 that they had all things in common instead of clinging to their private possessions. In the very next verse he adds, "*And with great power* the apostles gave their testimony to the resurrection of the Lord Jesus (v. 33, my emphasis). Jesus' prayer that the loving unity of his followers would be so striking that it would convince the world that he had come from the Father has been answered—at least once! It happened in the Jerusalem church. The unusual quality of their life together gave power to the apostolic preaching.

The account in Acts 6 is particularly instructive. Apparently there was a significant minority of Hellenists in the Jerusalem church. (Hellenists were Greek-speaking Jews, perhaps even Greeks that had converted to Judaism.) Somehow the Jewish speaking majority had overlooked the needs of the Hellenist widows until they complained about the injustice. The church's response is startling. The seven men chosen to look after this matter were all from the minority group! Every one of their names is Greek.[21] The church turned over their entire programme and funds for needy widows to the minority group that had been discriminated against. What was the result of this new act of financial fellowship? "*And the word of God increased;* and the number of the disciples multiplied greatly in Jerusalem" (Acts 6:7).

Redeemed economic relationships in the early church resulted in an increase of the Word of God. What a sobering thought! Is it perhaps the same today? Would similar economic changes produce a dramatic increase of believers today? Probably so. Are those who talk most glibly about the importance of evangelism prepared to pay *that* price?

But what is the price to be paid? What was the precise nature of the Jerusalem church's costly *koinonia*? The earliest church did not insist on absolute economic equality. Nor did they abolish private property. Peter reminded Ananias that he had been under no obligation either to sell his property or to donate the proceeds to the church (Acts 5:4). Sharing was voluntary, not compulsory.[22] But love for brothers and sisters was so overwhelming that many freely abandoned legitimate claims to private possessions. "No one said that any of the things which he possessed was his own" (Acts 4:32). That does not mean that everyone donated everything. Later in Acts we see that John Mark's mother, Mary, still owned her own house (Acts 12:12). Others also undoubtedly retained some private property.

The tense of the Greek words confirms this interpretation. Both in Acts 2:45 and 4:34, the verbs are in the imperfect tense. In Greek the imperfect tense denotes continued, repeated action over an extended period of time. Thus the meaning is, "They often sold possessions . . ." or, "They were in the habit of regularly bringing the proceeds of what was being sold."[23] The text does not suggest that the community decided to abolish all private property and everyone instantly sold everything. Rather it suggests that over a period of time, whenever there was need, believers regularly sold lands and houses to aid the needy.

What then was the essence of the transformed economic relationships in the Jerusalem church? The best way to describe their practice is to speak of unlimited liability and total availability. Their sharing was not superficial or occasional. Regularly and repeatedly, "they sold their possessions and goods and distributed them to all, *as any had need*." If the need was greater than current cash reserves, they sold property. They simply gave until the needs were met. The needs of the sister and brother, not legal property rights or future financial security, were decisive. They made their financial resources unconditionally available to each other. Oneness in Christ for the earliest Christian community meant unlimited economic liability for, and total economic availability to, the other members of Christ's body.

Unfortunately most Christians ignore the example of the Jerusalem church. Perhaps it is because of the economic self-interest of affluent Christians. At any rate, we have developed a convenient rationale for relegating the pattern of the Jerusalem church to the archivists' attic of irrelevant historical trivia. Why did Paul have to take a collection for the Jerusalem church a few decades later? A recent book offers the familiar response:

The trouble in Jerusalem was that they turned their capital into income, and had no cushion for hard times, and the Gentile Christians had to come to their rescue. It is possible not to live for bread alone, not to be overcome by materialist values, and at the same time to act responsibly; and this is why the Church may be grateful for the protest of the commune movement, but still consider that it has no answer.[24]

But were the Jerusalem Christians really irresponsible, naive communal-types whom we should respect but certainly not imitate? It is absolutely essential to insist that the Jerusalem principle of unlimited economic liability and total financial availability does not necessarily require communal living. It did not in Jerusalem! The Christian commune is only one of many faithful models. We dare not let the communal hobgoblin distort our discussion of the Jerusalem model.

But why did the Jerusalem church run into financial difficulty? It is quite unlikely that their economic sharing was to blame. Rather, it was due to a unique set of historical circumstances. Jerusalem attracted an unusually large number of poor. Since Jews considered alms given in Jerusalem particularly meritorious, the large numbers of pilgrims to the city were especially generous. As a result vast crowds of impoverished beggars flocked to the city.[25] In addition a disproportionately large number of older people gravitated to the Holy City to die or wait for the Messiah (see Lk. 2:25, 36).[26] There was also an unusually large number of rabbis living in Jerusalem because it was the centre of Jewish faith. Rabbis depended on charity, however, since they were not paid for teaching. Their students likewise were often poor. Hence the large number of religious scholars in Jerusalem swelled the ranks of the destitute.[27]

Nor was that all. Natural disasters struck at midcentury. The Roman historians Suetonius and Tacitus report recurring food shortages and famines during the reign of the Emperor Claudius (A.D. 41–54). Josephus dates such shortages in Palestine around A.D. 44–48.[28] Famine in Palestine was so severe at one point that the Antioch church quickly sent assistance (Acts 11:27–30).

There were also special reasons within the first church itself for unusual poverty. Jesus' particular concern for the poor and oppressed probably attracted a disproportionately large number of impoverished persons into the early church. Persecution must also have wreaked severe havoc with the normal income of Christians. Acts records considerable open persecution (Acts 8:1–3; 9:29; 12:1–5; 23:12–15). Undoubtedly Christians also experienced subtle forms of discrimination in many areas including employment.[29] Finally, the Twelve must have given up their livelihood when they moved from their native Galilee to Jerusalem. Hence their support increased the demand on the resources of the Jerusalem church.

These are some of the many reasons why the first community of Christians faced financial difficulty at midcentury. But misguided generosity was hardly a significant factor. In fact it was probably precisely the unusually large number of poor in their midst that made dramatic sharing such an obvious necessity. That the rich among them gave with overflowing generosity to meet a desperate need in the body of Christ indicates not naive idealism but unconditional discipleship.

The costly sharing of the first church stands as a constant challenge to Christians of all ages. They dared to give concrete, visible expression to the oneness of believers. In the new messianic community of Jesus' first followers after Pentecost, God was redeeming all relationships. The result was unconditional economic liability for and total financial availability to the other brothers and sisters in Christ.

Whatever the beauty and appeal of such an example, however, was it not a vision which quickly faded? Most people believe it was. But the actual practice of the early church proves the contrary.

ECONOMIC KOINONIA Paul broadened the vision of economic sharing among the people of God in a dramatic way. He devoted a great deal of time to raising money for Jewish Christians among Gentile congregations. In the process he developed *intra*church assistance (within one local church) into *inter*church sharing among all the scattered congregations of believers. From the time of the Exodus, God had taught his chosen people to exhibit transformed economic relations among themselves. With Peter and Paul, however, biblical religion moved beyond one ethnic group and became a universal, multiethnic faith. Paul's collection demonstrates that the oneness of that new body of believers entails economic sharing across ethnic and geographic lines.

Paul's concern for economic sharing in the body of Christ began early. Famine struck Palestine in A.D. 46. In response the believers at Antioch gave *"every one according to his ability* to send relief to the brethren who lived in Judea" (Acts 11:29, my emphasis). Paul helped Barnabas bring this economic assistance from Antioch to Jerusalem.[30]

That trip was just the beginning of Paul's extensive concern for economic sharing. For several years he devoted much time and energy to his great collection. He discusses his concern in several letters. Already in Galatians he expresses eagerness to assist the poor Jerusalem Christians (Gal. 2:10). He mentions it in the letter to Rome (Rom. 15:22–28). Briefly noted in 1 Corinthians 16:1–4, the collection became a major pre-occupation in 2 Corinthians 7—9. He also arranged for the collection in the churches of Macedonia, Galatia, Corinth, Ephesus and probably elsewhere.[31]

Paul knew he faced certain danger and possible death. But he still insisted on personally accompanying the offering. It was while delivering this financial assistance that Paul was arrested for the last time. His letter to the Romans shows that he was not blind to the danger (Rom. 15:31). Repeatedly friends and prophets warned Paul as he and the representatives of the contributing churches journeyed toward Jerusalem (Acts 21:4,

10–14). But Paul had a deep conviction that this financial symbol of Christian unity mattered far more even than his own life. "What are you doing, weeping and breaking my heart?" he chided friends imploring him not to accompany the others to Jerusalem. "For I am ready not only to be imprisoned but even to die at Jerusalem for the name of the Lord Jesus" (Acts 21:13). And he continued the journey. His passionate commitment to economic sharing with brothers and sisters led to his final arrest and martyrdom (see Acts 24:17).

Why was Paul so concerned with the financial problems of the Jerusalem church? Because of his understanding of fellowship. *Koinonia* is an extremely important concept in Paul's theology. And it is central in his discussion of the collection.

The word *koinonia* means fellowship with someone or participation in something. Believers enjoy fellowship with the Lord Jesus (1 Cor. 1:9).[32] Experiencing the *koinonia* of Jesus means having his righteousness imputed to us. It also entails sharing in the self-sacrificing, cross-bearing life he lived (Phil. 3:8–10). Nowhere is the Christian's fellowship with Christ experienced more powerfully than in the Eucharist. Sharing in the Lord's Supper draws the believer into a participation (*koinonia*) in the mystery of the cross: "The cup of blessing which we bless, is it not a participation (*koinonia*) in the blood of Christ? The bread which we break, is it not a participation (*koinonia*) in the body of Christ?" (1 Cor. 10:16).

Paul's immediate inference is that *koinonia* with Christ inevitably involves *koinonia* with all the members of the body of Christ. "Because there is one bread, we who are many are one body, for we all partake of the one bread" (1 Cor. 10:17; see also 1 Jn. 1:3–4). As seen in Ephesians 2, Christ's death for Jew and Gentile, male and female, has broken down all ethnic, sexual and cultural dividing walls. In Christ there is one new person, one new body of believers. When the brothers and sisters share the one bread and the common cup in the Lord's Supper, they symbolize and actualize their participation in the one body of Christ.

That is why the class divisions at Corinth so horrified Paul. Apparently wealthy Christians feasted at the eucharistic celebration while poor believers went hungry. Paul angrily denied that they were eating the Lord's Supper at all (1 Cor. 11:20–22). In fact they were profaning the Lord's body and blood because they did not discern his body (1 Cor. 11:27–29).

But what did Paul mean when he charged that they did not discern the Lord's body? To discern the Lord's body is to understand and live the truth that fellowship with Christ is inseparable from membership in his body where our oneness in Christ far transcends differences of race or class. Discernment of that one body of believers leads to unlimited availability to and responsibility for the other sisters and brothers. Discernment of that one body prompts us to weep with those who weep and rejoice with those who rejoice. Discernment of that one body is totally incompatible with feasting while other members of the body go hungry. Those who live a practical denial of their unity and fellowship in Christ, Paul insists, drink judgement on themselves when they go to the Lord's table. In fact they do not really partake of the Lord's Supper at all.

Once we understand the implication of Paul's teaching on discerning the body in the Lord's Supper, we dare not rest content until the scandal of starving Christians is removed. As long as any Christian anywhere in the world is hungry, the eucharistic celebration of all Christians everywhere in the world is imperfect.

For Paul, the intimate fellowship in the body of Christ has concrete economic implications for he uses precisely this same word, *koinonia*, to designate financial sharing among believers. Early in his ministry, the Jerusalem leaders endorsed his mission to the Gentiles after a dramatic debate. When they extended the "right hand of fellowship" (*koinonia*) they stipulated just one tangible expression of that fellowship. Paul promised financial assistance for his fellow Christians in Jerusalem (Gal. 2:9–10).[33]

Paul frequently employs the word *koinonia* as a virtual synonym for "collection." He speaks of the "liberality of the fellowship" (*koinonia*) that the Corinthians' generous offering would demonstrate (2 Cor. 9:13, see also 8:4).[34] He employed the same language to report the Macedonian Christians' offering for Jerusalem. It seemed good to the Macedonians "to make fellowship (*koinonia*) with the poor among the saints at Jerusalem" (Rom. 15:26). Indeed, this financial sharing was just one part of a total fellowship. The Gentile Christians had come to share in (he uses the verb form of *koinonia*) the spiritual blessings of the Jews. Therefore it was fitting for the Gentiles to share their material resources. Economic sharing was an obvious and crucial part of Christian fellowship for St. Paul.[35]

Paul's first guideline for sharing in the body of believers was general: Give all you can. Each person should give "as he may prosper" (1 Cor. 16:2). But that does not mean a small donation that costs nothing. Paul praised the Macedonians who "gave according to their means ... and beyond their means" (2 Cor. 8:3). The Macedonians were extremely poor. Apparently they faced particularly severe financial difficulties just when Paul asked for a generous offering (2 Cor. 8:2). But still they gave beyond their means! No hint here of a mechanical 10 per cent for pauper and millionaire. Giving as much as you can is the Pauline pattern.

Second, giving was voluntary (2 Cor. 8:3). Paul specifically noted that he was not issuing a command to the Corinthians (2 Cor. 8:8). Legalism is not the answer.

Paul's third guideline is the most startling. The norm, he suggests, is something like economic equality among the people of God. "I do not mean that others should be eased and you burdened, but that as a matter of equality your abundance at the present time should supply their want, so that their abundance may supply your want, that there may be equality." To support his principle, Paul quotes from the biblical story of the manna. "As it is written, 'He who gathered much had nothing over, and he who gathered little had no lack,'" (2 Cor. 8:13-15).

According to the Exodus account, when God started sending daily manna to the Israelites in the wilderness, Moses commanded the people to gather only as much as they needed for one day (Ex. 16:13-21). One omer (about four pints) per person would be enough, Moses said. Some greedy souls, however, apparently tried to gather more than they could use. But when they measured what they had gathered, they discovered that they all had just one omer per person. "He that gathered much had nothing over, and he that gathered little had no lack" (Ex. 16:18).

Paul quotes from the biblical account of the manna to support his guideline for economic sharing. Just as God had insisted on equal portions of manna for all his people in the wilderness, so now the Corinthians should give "that there may be equality" in the body of Christ.

This may be startling and disturbing to rich Christians in the Northern Hemisphere. But the biblical text clearly shows that Paul enunciates the principle of economic equality among the people of God to guide the Corinthians in their giving. *"It is a question of equality. At the moment your surplus meets their need, but one day your need may be met from their surplus. The aim is equality"* (NEB). [36]

It is exciting to see how the biblical teaching on transformed economic relationships among God's people created in the early church a concern for the poor which was unique in late antiquity. Writing about A.D. 125, the Christian philosopher Aristides painted the following picture of economic sharing in the church.

They walk in all humility and kindness, and falsehood is not found among them, and they love one another. They despise not the widow, and grieve not the orphan. He that hath, distributeth liberally to him that hath not. If they see a stranger, they bring him under their roof, and rejoice over him, as it were their own brother: for they call themselves brethren, not after the flesh, but after the spirit and in God; but when one of their poor passes away from the world, and any of them see him, then he provides for his burial according to his ability; and if they hear that any of their number is imprisoned or oppressed for the name of their Messiah, all of them provide for his needs, and if it is possible that he may be delivered, they deliver him. And if there is among them a man that is poor and needy, and they have not an abundance of necessaries, they fast two or three days that they may supply the needy with their necessary food.[37]

By A.D. 250 the church at Rome supported fifteen hundred needy persons. According to the German scholar Martin Hengel, this kind of economic sharing was unique in the late Roman Empire.[38]

That this transformed lifestyle made a powerful impression on outsiders is clear from a grudging comment by a pagan emperor. During his short reign (A.D. 361–363), Julian the Apostate tried to stamp out Christianity. But he was forced to admit to a fellow pagan "that the godless Galileans [Christians] feed not only their poor but ours also." With chagrin he acknowledged that the pagan cult which he had tried to revive had failed miserably in the task of aiding the poor.[39]

The practice of second-century Christians, however interesting it may be, is of course not normative today. In fact many would eagerly insist that neither is the practice of Paul at Corinth or the first Christians in Jerusalem. What relevance then does their economic sharing have for the contemporary church?

Certainly the church today need not slavishly imitate every detail of the life of the early church depicted in Acts. It is scriptural teaching, not the action of the Jerusalem church, that is normative. But that does not mean that we can simply dismiss the economic sharing described in Acts and the Pauline letters.

Over and over again God specifically commanded his people to live together in community in such a way that they would avoid extremes of wealth and poverty. That is the point of the legislation concerning the Jubilee and the sabbatical year. That is the point of the legislation on tithing, gleaning and loans. Jesus, our only perfect model, shared a common purse with the new community of his disciples. The first-century Christians were simply implementing what both the Old Testament and Jesus commanded.

The powerful evangelistic impact of the economic sharing at Jerusalem indicates that God approved and blessed the practice of the Jerusalem church. When in some places Scripture commands transformed economic relationships among God's people, and in other places describes God's blessing on his people as they implement these commands, then we can be sure that we have discovered a normative pattern for the church today.

What is striking, in fact, is the fundamental continuity of biblical teaching and practice at this point. The Bible repeatedly and pointedly reveals that God wills transformed economic relationships among his people. Paul's collection was simply an application of the basic principle of the Jubilee. The particular method, of course, was different because the people of God at his time were a multiethnic body living in different lands. But the principle was the same. Since the Greeks at Corinth were now part of the people of God, they were to share with the poor Jewish Christians at Jerusalem—that there might be equality!

CONCLUSION We have looked carefully at the kind of economic relationships God desires among his people. What does this biblical revelation mean for affluent Christians in the Northern Hemisphere? Only one conclusion seems possible to me.

Present economic relationships in the worldwide body of Christ are unbiblical, sinful, a hindrance to evangelism and a desecration of the body and blood of Jesus Christ. It is a sinful abomination for a small fraction of the world's Christians living in the Northern Hemisphere to grow richer year by year while our brothers and sisters in the Third World ache and suffer for lack of minimal health care, minimal education, and even just enough food to escape starvation.

We are like the rich Corinthian Christians who feasted without sharing their food with the poor members of the church (1 Cor. 11:20–29). Like them we fail today to discern the reality of the one worldwide body of Christ. The tragic consequence is that we profane the body and blood of the Lord Jesus we worship. Christians in the United States spent $5·7 billion on new church construction alone in the six years from 1967–72.[40] Would we go on building lavishly furnished expensive church plants if members of our own congregations were starving? Do we not flatly contradict Paul if we live as if African or Latin American members of the body of Christ are less a part of us than the members of our home congregation?[41]

Perhaps we ought to match every pound on new building with an additional pound above normal giving on the Lord's work overseas.

The present division between the haves and have-nots in the body of Christ is a major hindrance to world evangelism. Hungry people in the Third and Fourth Worlds find it difficult to accept a Christ preached by people who always symbolize (and often defend the affluence of) the richest societies on earth.

Lost opportunities and past and present sin, however, must not blind us to present potential. We live in a world dangerously divided between rich and poor. If a mere fraction of North American and European Christians would begin to apply biblical principles on economic sharing among the worldwide people of God, the world would be utterly astounded. There is probably no other step that would have such a powerful evangelistic impact today. Is it not likely that millions and millions of unbelievers would confess Christ? Jesus' prayer might be answered. The mutual love and unity within Christ's body might convince the world that Jesus indeed came from the Father (Jn. 17:20–23).

The church is the most universal body in the world today. It has the opportunity to live a new model of sharing at a crucial moment in world history. Because of its concern for the poor, the church in the past pioneered in developing schools and hospitals. Later, secular governments institutionalized the new models. In the late twentieth century, a dangerously divided, global village awaits a new model of economic sharing.

The Bible clearly teaches that God wills fundamentally transformed economic relationships among his people. Do we have the faith and obedience to start living the biblical vision?

A BIBLICAL ATTITUDE TOWARDS PROPERTY & WEALTH

IN THE HOUSE OF THE RIGHTEOUS THERE IS MUCH TREASURE. [PROV. 15:6] BLESSED ARE YOU POOR, FOR YOURS IS THE KINGDOM OF GOD. [LK. 6:20]

The title of this chapter, "A Biblical Attitude toward Property and Wealth", promptly suggests an important question: Does the Bible sanction or condemn private property? Unfortunately for many this is the only important question raised by the title. The biblical viewpoint is strikingly different. The Bible teaches many things about property and wealth.

PRIVATE PROPERTY The Ten Commandments sanction private property implicitly and explicitly.[1] God forbids stealing, indeed even coveting, the house, land or animals of one's neighbours (Ex. 20:15, 17; Deut. 5:19, 21; see also Deut. 27:17; Prov. 22:28). Apparently Jesus likewise assumed the legitimacy of private property. His disciple, Simon Peter, owned a house that Jesus frequented (Mk. 1:29). Jesus commanded his followers to give to the poor (Mt. 6:2–4) and loan money even when there was no reasonable hope of repayment (Mt. 5:42; Lk. 6:34–35). Such advice would have made little sense if Jesus had not also assumed that the possession of property and money was legitimate so that one could make loans. As we saw in the previous chapter, not even the dramatic economic sharing in the first Jerusalem church led to a rejection of private ownership. Throughout biblical revelation, the legitimacy of private property is constantly affirmed.[2]

But the right of private property is not absolute. From the perspective of biblical revelation, property owners are not free to seek their own profit without regard for the needs of the neighbour. Such an outlook derives from the secular laissez-faire economics of the Scottish deist Adam Smith, not from Scripture.

Smith published a book in 1776 which has profoundly shaped Western society in the last two centuries.[3] (Since the Keynesian revolution, of course, Smith's ideas have shaped Western societies less than previously, but his fundamental outlook, albeit in somewhat revised form, still provides the basic ideological framework for many people in the West.) Smith argued that an invisible hand would guarantee the good of all if each person would pursue his or her own economic self-interest in the context of a competitive society. Supply and demand for goods and services must be the sole determinant of prices and wages. If the law of supply and demand reigns and if all seek their own advantage within a competitive, non-monopolistic economy, the good of society will be served. Owners of land and capital therefore have not only the right but also the obligation to seek as much profit as possible.

Such an outlook may be extremely attractive to successful people in the Western World. Indeed laissez-faire economics has been espoused by some as *the* Christian economics. In reality, however, it is a product of the Enlightenment. It reflects a modern, secularized outlook rather than a biblical perspective.

It is interesting to note the striking parallel between the laissez-faire and the pagan Roman attitude toward private property. Carl F. H. Henry, former editor of *Christianity Today*, rightly contrasts the biblical and Roman understanding: "The Roman or Justinian view derives ownership from natural right; it defines ownership as the individual's unconditional and exclusive power over property. It implies an owner's right to use property as he pleases ... irrespective of the will of others." And Henry admits that this pagan view "still remains the silent presupposition of much of the free world's common practice today."[4]

According to biblical faith, Yahweh is Lord of all things. He is the sovereign Lord of history. Economics is not a neutral, secular sphere independent of his lordship. Economic activity, like every other area of life, should be subject to his will and revelation.

How does the biblical view that Yahweh is Lord of all of life require a modification of the laissez-faire belief that the right of private property is absolute and inviolable? The Bible insists that God alone has an absolute right to property. Furthermore, it teaches that this Absolute Owner places significant limitations on how his people acquire and use his property.

The psalmist summarized the biblical view of Yahweh's absolute ownership: "The earth is the LORD's and the fullness thereof, the world and those who dwell therein" (Ps. 24:1). "Whatever is under the whole heaven is mine," God informed Job (Job 41:11; see also Ps. 50:12; Deut. 26:10; Ex. 19:5). In the last chapter we examined the year of Jubilee. It is precisely because absolute ownership of the land rested with Yahweh rather than the Israelite farmers that he could command the redistribution of land every fiftieth year: "The land shall not be sold in perpetuity, *for the land is mine;* for you are strangers and sojourners with me" (Lev. 25:23, my emphasis; see also Deut. 10:14). Because he is the creator and sustainer of all things, God alone has absolute property rights.

As absolute owner, God places limitations on the acquisition and use of property. According to the Old Testament, "the right to property was in principle subordinated to the obligation to care for the weaker members of society."[5] That is the clear implication of the legislation, discussed in the last chapter, on the Jubilee, the sabbatical year, gleaning and interest. Property owners did not have the right to harvest everything in their fields. They were to leave some for the poor. When an Israelite farmer purchased land, he really only bought the use of the land until the year of Jubilee (Lev. 25:15-17). Indeed even the right to use the land for the intervening years was not absolute. If a relative of the seller appeared, the purchaser had to sell the land back promptly. Or if the seller recovered financial solvency, he had the right to buy back his land immediately (Lev. 25:25–28). The purchaser's right of ownership was subordinate to the original owner's right to earn a living.

God was concerned to avoid extremes of wealth and poverty among his people. He wanted each family to possess the means to earn its own way. These human rights, even of the less advantaged who regularly fell behind the more aggressive, more prosperous persons, were more significant than the property rights of the person able to pay the market price for land. Thus the rights of the poor and disadvantaged to possess the means to earn a just living have precedence over the rights of the more prosperous to make a profit (Nehemiah 5).

This attitude toward property stems from the high view of persons held in Israel. Old Testament scholars have pointed out that Israel, unlike other ancient civilizations such as Babylon, Assyria and Egypt, considered all citizens equal before the law. In other societies the social status of the offender (royal official, poor man, priest) determined how his offence was judged and punished. In Israel all citizens were equal before the law. Because of this high view of persons, property seemed less significant by comparison.

This equality before the law is accompanied by a new respect for human life. Whereas in neighbouring states offences connected with property such as theft, robbery, etc., were frequently punished with the death penalty, this was no longer the case in the law of the Old Testament. The life of even the most degraded person is worth more than the richest possession.[6]

The case of slaves illustrates this point. In all other ancient civilizations slaves were viewed as mere property. The owner was completely free to treat the slave according to his whim. But in Israel the slave was a person, not a piece of property. Specific laws guaranteed him certain rights (Ex. 21:20, 26, 27; Deut. 23:15–16). "The fact that, in accordance with God's order, the life of every individual, even of the poorest, is of greater value than all material things—this fact represents an insurmountable stumbling-block to all economic developments which make profits for the few out of human misery."[7]

A CAREFREE ATTITUDE TOWARD POSSESSIONS

Jesus calls his followers to a joyful life of carefree unconcern for possessions:

I bid you put away anxious thoughts about food to keep you alive and clothes to cover your body. Life is more than food, the body more than clothes. Think of the ravens: they neither sow nor reap; they have no storehouse or barn; yet God feeds them. You are worth far more than the birds! Is there a man among you who by anxious thought can add a foot to his height? If, then, you cannot do even a very little thing, why are you anxious about the rest?

Think of the lilies: they neither spin nor weave; yet I tell you, even Solomon in all his splendour was not attired like one of these. But if that is how God clothes the grass, which is growing in the field today, and tomorrow is thrown on the stove, how much more will he clothe you! How little faith you have! And so you are not to set your mind on food and drink; you are not to worry. For all these are things for the heathen to run after; but you have a Father who knows that you need them. No, set your mind upon his kingdom, and all the rest will come to you as well. (Lk. 12:22–31, NEB; see also 2 Cor. 9:8–11)

Jesus' words are anathema to Marxists and capitalists alike: to Marxists because they worship Mammon by claiming that economic forces are the ultimate causal factors in history; to capitalists because they worship Mammon by idolizing economic success as the highest good.[8] Indeed, at another level, Jesus' words are anathema to the ordinary, comfortable "Christian." In fact I must confess that I cannot read them without an underlying sense of uneasiness. The beauty and appeal of the passage always overwhelms me. But it also always reminds me that I have not, in spite of continuing struggle and effort, attained the kind of carefree attitude Jesus depicts.

What is the secret of such carefree living? First, many people cling to their possessions instead of sharing them because they are worried about the future. But is not such an attitude finally unbelief? If we really believe that God is who Jesus said he is, then we can begin to live without anxiety for the future. Jesus taught us that God is our loving Father. His word *Abba* (Mk. 14:36) is a tender, intimate word like *Papa*. If we really believe that the almighty creator and sustainer of the cosmos is our loving Papa, then we can begin to cast aside anxiety about earthly possessions.

Second, such carefree living is an unconditional commitment to Jesus as Lord. We must genuinely want to seek first the kingdom of heaven. Jesus was very blunt. We cannot serve God and possessions. "No one can serve two masters; for either he will hate the one and love the other, or he will be devoted to the one and despise the other. You cannot serve God and Mammon" (Mt. 6:24). Mammon is not some mysterious pagan God. The word *mammon* is simply the Aramaic word for wealth or property.[9] Like the rich young ruler and Zacchaeus, we must decide between Jesus and riches. Like the merchant in Jesus' parable, we must decide between the kingdom of heaven and our affluent life: "The kingdom of heaven is like a merchant in search of fine pearls, who, on finding one pearl of great value, went and sold all that he had and bought it" (Mt. 13:45, 46; see also v. 44). Either Jesus and his kingdom matter so much that we are ready to sacrifice everything else, including our possessions, or we are not serious about Jesus.

If Jesus is truly Lord and if we trust in a loving heavenly Father, then we can take courage to live without anxiety about possessions. That kind of carefree unconcern for possessions, however, is not merely an inner spiritual attitude. It involves concrete action. Immediately following the moving statement about the carefree life of the ravens and lilies, Jesus says, "Sell your possessions, and give alms; provide yourselves with purses that do not grow old, with a treasure in the heavens that does not fail ... For where your treasure is, there will your heart be also" (Lk. 12:33–34).

If there are poor people who need assistance, Jesus' carefree disciple will help—even if that means selling possessions. People are vastly more important than property. "Laying up treasure in heaven" means exactly the same thing. "In Jewish literature, the good deeds of a religious person are often described as treasures stored up in heaven."[10] One stores up treasure in heaven by doing righteousness on earth. And aiding the poor is one of the most basic acts of righteousness. Jesus does not mean, of course, that we earn salvation by assisting the needy. But he does mean to urge his followers to be so unconcerned with property that they eagerly sell it to aid the poor and oppressed. Such activity is an integral part of living a life of joyful unconcern for possessions.

But a difficult question remains. Did Jesus mean that we should sell all our possessions? How literally should we understand what he said in Luke 6:30: "Give to every one who begs from you, and of him who takes away your goods do not ask them again"? Jesus sometimes engaged in typical Jewish hyperbole to make a point. He hardly meant in Luke 14:26 that one must actively hate father and mother in order to be his disciple. But we have become so familiar with Jesus' words and so accustomed to compromising their call to radical discipleship and unconditional commitment that we weaken his real intent. What 99 per cent of all Western Christians need to hear 99 per cent of the time is: "Give to everyone who begs from you", and "sell your possessions". It is certainly true that Jesus' followers continued to own some private property. But Jesus clearly taught that the kind of substantial sharing he desired would involve selling possessions. His first followers at Jerusalem took him very seriously. If Christians today in affluent countries want to experience Jesus' carefree outlook on property and possessions, they will need to do the same.

Other parts of the New Testament continue the same theme. Bishops must not be lovers of money (1 Tim. 3:3; Tit. 1:7). Deacons likewise dare not be "greedy for gain" (1 Tim. 3:8). In many churches today, "success" in business is one of the chief criteria for selection to the church board. Is that not a blatant reversal of biblical teaching on the importance of possessions? Even those who are rich should be careful not to set their hope in "uncertain riches". Instead, they should trust in God and share generously (1 Tim. 6:17–18). "Keep your life free from love of money, and be content with what you have; for he has said, 'I will never fail you nor forsake you'" (Heb. 13:5). Our future is secure not because of our possessions but because it rests in the hands of a loving, omnipotent Father. If we truly trust in him and are unconditionally submitted to his lordship, we can confidently imitate Jesus' carefree unconcern for property and possessions.

THE RICH FOOL Most Christians in the Northern Hemisphere simply do not believe Jesus' teaching about the deadly danger of possessions. We all know that Jesus warned that possessions are highly dangerous—so dangerous in fact that it is extremely difficult for a rich person to be a Christian at all. "It is easier for a camel to go through the eye of a needle than for a rich man to enter the kingdom of God" (Lk. 18:24, 25). But we do not believe Jesus. We Christians in the West live in the richest society in the history of the world surrounded by a billion hungry neighbours. Yet we demand that our governments foster an ever-expanding economy in order that our incomes will increase each year. We insist on more and more. If Jesus was so unlike us that he considered riches dangerous, then we must ignore or reinterpret his message.

But he said it all the same. Matthew, Mark and Luke all record the terrible warning: "How hard it is for those who have riches to enter the kingdom of God!" (Lk, 18:24; Mk. 10:23; Mt. 19:23). The context of this saying shows why possessions are dangerous. Jesus spoke these words to his disciples immediately after the rich young man had decided to cling to his wealth rather than follow Jesus (Lk. 18:18–23). Riches are dangerous because their seductive power very frequently persuades us to reject Jesus and his kingdom.

The sixth chapter of 1 Timothy underlines and reinforces Jesus' teaching. Christians should be content with the necessities of food and clothing (1 Tim. 6:8). Why?

Those who desire to be rich fall into temptation, into a snare, into many senseless and hurtful desires that plunge men into ruin and destruction. For the love of money is the root of all evils; it is through this craving that some have wandered away from the faith and pierced their hearts with many pangs. (1 Tim. 6:9–10)

A desire for riches prompts people to do anything for the sake of economic success. The result, Scripture warns, is anguish now and damnation later.

That economic success tempts people to forget God was already a biblical theme in the Old Testament. Before they entered the promised land, God warned the people of Israel about the danger of riches.

Take heed lest you forget the LORD your God . . . lest when you have eaten and are full, and have built goodly houses and live in them, and when your herds and flocks multiply, and your silver and gold is multiplied, and all that you have is multiplied, then your heart be lifted up, and you forget the LORD your God . . . Beware lest you say in your heart, "My power and the might of my hand have gotten me this wealth." (Deut. 8 :11–17)

An abundance of possessions can easily lead us to forget that God is the source of all good. We trust in ourselves and our wealth rather than in the Almighty.

Not only do possessions tempt us to forsake God. War and neglect of the poor often result from the pursuit of wealth. "What causes wars and what causes fightings among you? . . . You desire and do not have; so you kill. And you covet and cannot obtain; so you fight and wage war" (Jas. 4:1–2). A cursory reading of world history confirms this point.

Instead of fostering more compassion toward the poor, riches often harden the hearts of the wealthy. Scripture is full of instances in which rich persons are unconcerned about the poor at their doorstep (Lk. 16:19–31; Is. 5:8–10; Amos 6:4–7; Jas. 5:1–5). Dom Helder Camara, a Brazilian archbishop who has devoted his life to seeking justice for the poor, makes the point forcefully:

I used to think, when I was a child, that Christ might have been exaggerating when he warned about the dangers of wealth. Today I know better. I know how very hard it is to be rich and still keep the milk of human kindness. Money has a dangerous way of putting scales on one's eyes, a dangerous way of freezing people's hands, eyes, lips and hearts.[11]

Possessions are positively dangerous because they often encourage unconcern for the poor, because they lead to strife and war, and because they seduce people into forsaking God.

The usage of the word *covetousness* (it occurs nineteen times in the New Testament) reflects the biblical understanding of the dangers of riches. The Greek word *pleonexia* (translated "covetousness") means "striving for material possessions".[12]

Jesus's parable of the rich fool vividly portrays the nature of covetousness. When a man came running to Jesus for help in obtaining his share of a family inheritance, Jesus refused to consider the case. Perceiving the real problem, Jesus warned instead of the danger of covetousness. "Take heed, and beware of all covetousness [*pleonexia*]; for man's life does not consist in the abundance of his possessions (Lk. 12:15). Knowing that the man was obsessed with material things, Jesus told him a story about a rich fool.

The land of a rich man brought forth plentifully; and he thought to himself, "What shall I do, for I have nowhere to store my crops?" And he said, "I will do this: I will pull down my barns, and build larger ones; and there I will store all my grain and my goods. And I will say to my soul, Soul, you have ample goods laid up for many years; take your ease, eat, drink, be merry." But God said to him, "Fool! This night your soul is required of you; and the things you have prepared, whose will they be?" So is he who lays up treasure for himself, and is not rich toward God. (Lk. 12:16–21)

The rich fool is the epitome of the covetous person. He has a greedy compulsion to acquire more and more possessions even though he does not need them. And his phenomenal success at piling up more and more property and wealth leads to the blasphemous conclusion that material possessions can satisfy all his needs. From the divine perspective, however, this attitude is sheer madness. He is a raving fool.

One cannot read the parable of the rich fool without thinking of our own society. We madly multiply more sophisticated gadgets, larger and taller buildings and faster means of transportation not because such things truly enrich our lives but because we are driven by an obsession for more and more. Covetousness—a striving for more and more material possessions—has become a cardinal vice of Western civilization.

The New Testament has a great deal to say about covetousness. It is divine punishment for sin. In its essence, it is idolatry. Scripture teaches that greedy persons must be expelled from the church. Certainly no covetous person will inherit the kingdom.

In Romans 1 Paul indicates that God sometimes punishes sin by letting sinners experience the ever more destructive consequences of their continuing rebellion against him. "And since they did not see fit to acknowledge God, God gave them up to a base mind and to improper conduct They were filled with all manner of wickedness, evil, *covetousness*, . . . murder, strife, deceit . . ." (Rom. 1:28–29, my emphasis). Covetousness is one of the sins with which God punishes our rebellion. The parable of the rich fool suggests how the punishment works out. Since we are made for communion with the Creator, we cannot obtain genuine fulfilment when we seek it in material possessions. Hence we seek ever more frantically and desperately for more and more houses and barns. Eventually we worship our possessions. As Paul indicates, covetousness is finally sheer idolatry (Eph. 5:5; Col. 3:5).

Paul actually commanded the Corinthians to exercise church discipline against covetous persons (1 Cor. 5:11). Christians today are not at all surprised that he urged the Corinthians to excommunicate a church member living with his father's wife (1 Cor. 5:1–5). But we quietly overlook the fact that Paul went right on (1 Cor. 5:11) to urge Christians not to associate with or even eat meals with persons who claim to be Christians but who are guilty of greed! Are we not guilty of covetousness when we demand an ever higher standard of living while a billion hungry neighbours starve? Is it not time for the church to begin applying church discipline to those guilty of this sin?[13] Would it not be more biblical to apply church discipline to people whose greedy acquisitiveness has led to "financial success" than to elect them to the board of elders?

Such action may be the last means we have of communicating the biblical warning that greedy persons will not inherit the kingdom.

Do you not know that the unrighteous will not inherit the kingdom of God? Do not be deceived; neither the immoral, nor idolators, nor adulterers, nor homosexuals, nor thieves, nor the greedy [the covetous], nor drunkards, nor revilers, nor robbers will inherit the kingdom of God. (1 Cor. 6:9–10, my emphasis)
Covetousness is just as sinful as idolatry and adultery.

The same vigorous, unambiguous word appears in Ephesians: "Be sure of this, that no fornicator or impure man, or one who is covetous (that is, an idolator), has any inheritance in the kingdom of Christ" (Eph. 5:5). These biblical passages should drive us all to our knees. I am afraid that I have been repeatedly and sinfully covetous. The same is true of the vast majority of Western Christians.

Possessions are highly dangerous. They lead to a multitude of sins, including idolatry. Western Christians today desperately need to turn away from their covetous civilization's grasping materialism.

THE RING AND THE BELOVED Possessions are dangerous. But they are not innately evil.[14] Biblical revelation begins with creation. And created things, God said, are very very good (Gen. 1).

Biblical faith knows nothing of the ascetic notion that forsaking food, possessions or sex is inherently virtuous. To be sure these created goods are, as St. Augustine said, only rings from our Beloved. They are not the Beloved himself. Sometimes particular circumstances—such as an urgent mission or the needs of the poor—may require their renunciation. But these things are part of God's good creation. Like the ring given by the Beloved, they are signs of his love. If we treasure them as good tokens of his affection instead of mistaking them for the Beloved, they are marvellous gifts which enrich our lives.

God's provision for Israel's use of the tithe symbolizes the scriptural perspective (Deut. 14:22–27). Every third year, as we saw earlier, the tithe was given to the poor. In the other years, however, the people were to go to the place of worship and have a fantastic feast. They were to have a great, big, joyful celebration! "Before the LORD your God, in the place which he will choose, to make his name dwell there, you shall eat the tithe of your grain, of your wine, and of your oil, and the firstlings of your herd and flock" (Deut. 14:23). Those who lived far from the place of worship could sell the tithe of their produce and take the money with them. Listen to God's directions for the party: "Spend the money for whatever you desire, oxen, or sheep, or wine or strong drink, whatever your appetite craves; and you shall eat there before the LORD your God and rejoice" (Deut. 14:26). God wants his people to celebrate the glorious goodness of his creation.

Jesus' example fits in perfectly with the Old Testament view. Certainly he said a great deal about the danger of possessions.

But he was not an ascetic. He was happy to join in marriage celebrations and even contribute the beverage (Jn. 2:1–11). He dined with the prosperous. Apparently he was sufficiently fond of feasts and celebrations that his enemies could spread the false rumour that he was a glutton and a drunkard (Mt. 11:19). Christian asceticism has a long history, but Jesus' life undermines its basic assumptions.

A short passage in 1 Timothy succinctly summarizes the biblical view. In the latter days people will forbid marriage and advocate abstinence from foods. But this is misguided, "for everything created by God is good, and nothing is to be neglected if it is received with thanksgiving" (1 Tim. 4:1–4).

The biblical teaching on the goodness of creation does not contradict the other biblical themes we have explored. It is also true that possessions are dangerous and that God's people must practice self-denial to aid the poor and feed the hungry. But it is important to focus the biblical mandate to liberate the poor without distorting other aspects of Scripture. It is not because food, clothes and property are inherently evil that Christians today must lower their standard of living. It is because others are starving. Creation is good. But the one who gave us this gorgeous token of his affection has asked us to share it with our sisters and brothers.

RIGHTEOUSNESS AND RICHES Does obedience guarantee prosperity? Is it true that "in the house of the righteous there is much treasure" (Prov. 15:6)? Is the reverse also true? Are riches a sure sign of righteousness?

The Bible certainly does not romanticize poverty. It is a curse (2 Sam. 3:29; Ps. 109:8–11). Sometimes it is the result of sin, but not always. A fundamental point of the book of Job is that poverty and suffering are not always due to disobedience. In fact they can be redemptive (Is. 53). Even so, poverty and suffering are not inherently good. They are tragic distortions of God's good creation.

Prosperity on the other hand is good and desirable. God repeatedly promised his people Israel that obedience would bring abundant prosperity in a land flowing with milk and honey (Deut. 6:1–3).

All these blessings shall come upon you . . . if you obey the voice of the LORD your God. . . . And the LORD will make you abound in prosperity, in the fruit of your body, and in the fruit of your cattle, and in the fruit of your ground. (Duet. 28 :2, 11 ; see also Deut. 7 :12–15)

That God frequently rewards obedience with material abundance is a clear teaching of Scripture.

But the threat of a curse always accompanied the promise of blessing (Deut. 6:14–15; 28:15–68; 8:11–20). As we discovered in the last two chapters, one of God's most frequent commands to his people was to feed the hungry and to bring justice to the poor and oppressed. For repeatedly ignoring this command, Israel experienced God's curse. Israel's prosperity in the days of Amos and Isaiah was not the result of divine blessing. It was the result of sinful oppression of the poor. God consequently destroyed the nation.

The Bible does teach that God rewards obedience with prosperity. But it denies the converse. It is a heresy, particularly common in the West, to think that wealth and prosperity are always a sure sign of righteousness. They may be the result of sin and oppression as in the case of Israel.[15] The crucial test is whether the prosperous are obeying God's command to bring justice to the oppressed. If they are not, they are living in damnable disobedience to God. On biblical grounds, therefore, one can be sure that prosperity in the context of injustice results from oppression rather than obedience, and is not a sign of righteousness.

The connection between righteousness, prosperity and concern for the poor is explicitly taught in Scripture. The picture of the "good wife" in Proverbs 31 provides one beautiful illustration. She is a diligent businesswoman who buys fields and engages in trade (vv. 14, 16, 18). She is a righteous woman who fears the Lord (v. 30). Her obedience and diligence clearly bring prosperity. But material possessions do not harden her heart against the poor: "She opens her hand to the poor, and reaches out her hands to the needy" (v. 20).

Psalm 112 is equally explicit:

> *Blessed is the man who fears the LORD,*
> *who greatly delights in his commandments! . . .*

> *Wealth and riches are in his house. . . .*
> *the LORD is gracious, merciful, and righteous.*
> *It is well with the man who deals generously and lends,*
> *who conducts his affairs with justice. . . .*
> *He has distributed freely, he has given to the poor.*
> *(Ps. 112:1, 3–5, 9)*

The righteous person distributes his riches freely to the poor. He works to establish justice for the oppressed. That kind of life is a sign that one's prosperity results from obedience rather than oppression.

God wills prosperity with justice. But that does not mean that wealthy persons who make Christmas baskets and give to relief have satisfied God's demand. God wills justice for the poor. And justice, as we have seen, means things like the Jubilee and the sabbatical remission of debts. It means economic structures that check the emergence of extremes of wealth and poverty. It means massive economic sharing among the people of God. Prosperity without that kind of biblical concern for justice unambiguously signifies disobedience.

We have seen that the Old Testament teaches that material possessions sometimes result from divine blessing. But is this view compatible with Jesus saying: "Blessed are you poor, for yours is the kingdom of God" (Lk. 6:20)? Does Jesus consider poverty itself a virtue? Furthermore, how can one reconcile the Lucan version of this beatitude with Matthew's version: "Blessed are the poor *in spirit*" (Mt. 5:3)?

The development of the idea of the "pious poor" in the centuries just prior to Christ helps answer these questions. Already in the Psalms the poor were often identified as the special objects of God's favour and protection precisely because they were oppressed by the wicked rich (see, for example, Psalm 8).[16] When Greece and then Rome conquered Palestine, Hellenistic culture and values were foisted upon the Jews. Those who remained faithful to Yahweh often suffered financially. Thus the term *poor* came to be used to describe faithful Jews. "It was virtually equivalent to pious, God-fearing, and godly and reflects a situation where the rich were mainly those who had sold out to the incoming culture and had allowed their religious devotion to become corrupted by the new ways. If the poor were the pious, the faithful and largely oppressed, the rich were the powerful, ungodly, worldly, even apostate."[17]

In such a setting the righteous are often poor, hungry and sad, not just "in spirit" but in reality. Matthew has not "spiritualized" Jesus' words. He has simply captured another aspect of Jesus' original meaning. Jesus was talking about those faithful persons who so hungered for righteousness that they sacrificed even their material prosperity when that became necessary. Jesus then did not mean that poverty and hunger are desirable in themselves. But in a sinful world where frequently success and prosperity are possible only if one transgresses God's law, poverty and hunger are indeed a blessing. The kingdom is for precisely such people.

Jesus' comment in Mark 10:29-30 adds further clarification. He promised that those who forsake all for the kingdom will receive a hundredfold even in this life. And he even included houses and lands, part of the good creation intended for our enjoyment. In the same sentence, however, he also promised persecution! Sometimes—perhaps most of the time—the wicked, powerful and rich will persecute those who dare to follow Jesus' teaching without compromise. Hunger and poverty often result. In such a time the poor and hungry disciples are indeed blessed.

I fear that we may be at the threshold of such an age. The time may soon come when those who dare to preach and live what the Bible teaches about the poor and possessions will experience terrible persecution. If the wars of redistribution envisaged by Heilbroner[18] become a reality, if affluent lands go to war to protect their unfair share of the world's food and resources, then persecution in affluent countries will inevitably occur.

In such an age faithful Christians will continue to assert that property rights are not absolute. They will courageously insist that the right of individuals and nations to use land and resources as they please is subordinate to the right of all people to eat and to earn a just living. They will understand more profoundly than today Jesus' carefree unconcern for possessions. As they see fellow church members choose security and affluence rather than faithfulness and persecution, they will realize how dangerous indeed are possessions and wealth. Certainly they will not despise the good gifts of creation. But when forced to choose between possessions and the kingdom, they will gladly forsake the ring for the Beloved.

STRUCTURAL EVIL & WORLD HUNGER

COME NOW, YOU RICH, WEEP AND HOWL FOR THE MISERIES THAT ARE COMING UPON YOU. YOUR RICHES HAVE ROTTED AND YOUR GARMENTS ARE MOTH-EATEN. YOUR GOLD AND SILVER HAVE RUSTED, AND THEIR RUST WILL BE EVIDENCE AGAINST YOU AND WILL EAT YOUR FLESH LIKE FIRE. YOU HAVE LAID UP TREASURE FOR THE LAST DAYS. BEHOLD, THE WAGES OF THE LABOURERS WHO MOWED YOUR FIELDS, WHICH YOU KEPT BACK BY FRAUD, CRY OUT; AND THE CRIES OF THE HARVESTERS HAVE REACHED THE EARS OF THE LORD OF HOSTS. YOU HAVE LIVED ON THE EARTH IN LUXURY AND IN PLEASURE; YOU HAVE FATTENED YOUR HEARTS IN A DAY OF SLAUGHTER. [JAMES 5:1-5]

I READ SOMETIME AGO THAT UPTON SINCLAIR, THE AUTHOR, READ THIS PASSAGE (JAMES 5:1-5) ... TO A GROUP OF MINISTERS. THEN HE ATTRIBUTED THE PASSAGE TO EMMA GOLDMAN, WHO AT THE TIME WAS AN ANARCHIST AGITATOR. THE MINISTERS WERE INDIGNANT, AND THEIR RESPONSE WAS, "THIS WOMAN OUGHT TO BE DEPORTED AT ONCE!" [UNPUBLISHED

In the early 1950s Northeast High School in Philadelphia was famous for its superb academic standards and its brilliant, long-standing athletic triumphs. The second oldest school in the city, Northeast had excellent teachers and a great tradition. And it was almost entirely white. Then in the midfifties, the neighbourhood began to change. Black people moved in. Whites began to flee in droves to the Greater Northeast, a new, all-white section of Philadelphia. Quite naturally, a new high school became necessary much further out in this developing overwhelmingly white area.

When the excellent new school was completed in 1957, the new school took along the name, Northeast High School, with its fond memories and traditions and many connotations of academic excellence and athletic triumph. The inner city school was renamed Edison High. The new school took all the academic and athletic trophies and awards, school colours and songs, powerful alumni and all the money in the treasury. Worst of all, the teachers were given the option of transferring to new Northeast High. Two-thirds of them did.[1]

The black students who now attended Edison High had an old, rapidly deteriorating building, frequent substitute teachers and no traditions. Nor did the intervening years bring many better teachers or adequate teaching materials. The academic record since 1957 has been terrible. In fact Edison High has only one claim to uniqueness. It has one national record. More students from Edison High died in Vietnam than from any other high school in the United States!

Who was guilty of this terrible sin? Local, state and federal politicians who had promoted *de facto* housing segregation for decades? The school board? Parents who had, at best, a very partial picture of what was going on? Christian community leaders? White students at the new Northeast High whose excellent education and job prospects have been possible, in part, precisely because of the poor facilities and bad teachers left behind for the black students at Edison? Who was guilty?

Many would deny any personal responsibility. "That's just the way things are." And they would be quite right! Long-standing patterns in jobs and housing had created a system which automatically produced Edison High. But that hardly silences the query about responsibility. Do we sin when we participate in evil social systems and societal structures that unfairly benefit some and harm others?

THE BIBLE AND STRUCTURAL EVIL Neglect of the biblical teaching on structural injustice or institutionalized evil is one of the most deadly omissions in evangelicalism today. What does the Bible say about structural evil and how does that deepen our understanding of the scriptural perspective on poverty and hunger?

Christians frequently restrict the scope of ethics to a narrow class of "personal" sins. A few years ago in a study of over fifteen hundred ministers, researchers discovered that the theologically conservative pastors speak out on sins such as drug abuse and sexual misconduct.[2] But they fail to preach about the sins of institutionalized racism, unjust economic structures and militaristic institutions which destroy people just as much as do alcohol and drugs.

There is an important difference between consciously willed, individual acts (like lying to a friend or committing an act of adultery) and participation in evil social structures. Slavery is an example of the latter. So is the Victorian factory system where ten-year-old children worked twelve to sixteen hours a day. Both slavery and child labour were legal. But they destroyed people by the millions. They were institutionalized or structural evils. In the twentieth century, as opposed to the nineteenth, evangelicals have been more concerned with individual sinful acts than with their participation in evil social structures.

But the Bible condemns both. Speaking through his prophet, Amos, the LORD declared,

For three transgressions of Israel, and for four, I will not revoke the punishment; because they sell the righteous for silver, and the needy for a pair of shoes—they that trample the head of the poor into the dust of the earth, and turn aside the way of the afflicted; a

man and his father go in to the same maiden, so that my holy name is profaned. (Amos 2 :6–7)

Biblical scholars have shown that some kind of legal fiction underlies the phrase "selling the needy for a pair of shoes."³ This mistreatment of the poor was *legal*! In one breath God condemns both sexual misconduct and legalized oppression of the poor. Sexual sins and economic injustice are equally displeasing to God.

God revealed the same thing through his prophet Isaiah:

Woe to those who join house to house, who add field to field, until there is no more room, and you are made to dwell alone in the midst of the land. The LORD of hosts has sworn in my hearing : "Surely many houses shall be desolate, large and beautiful houses, without inhabitant . . . Woe to those who rise early in the morning, that they may run after strong drink, who tarry late into the evening till wine inflames them!" (Is. 5 :8–11)

Equally powerful is the succinct, satirical summary in verses 22 and 23 of the same chapter: "Woe to those who are heroes at drinking wine, and valiant men in mixing strong drink, who acquit the guilty for a bribe, and deprive the innocent of his right." Here God condemns in one breath both the wealthy who amass large landholdings at the expense of the poor and also those who have fallen into drunkenness. Great economic inequality is just as abominable to our just God as drunkenness.

Some young activists have supposed that as long as they were fighting for the rights of minorities and opposing militarism, they were morally righteous regardless of how often they shacked up for the night with a girl in the movement. Some of their elders, on the other hand, have supposed that because they did not smoke, drink and lie, they were morally upright even though they lived in segregated communities and owned stock in companies that exploit the poor of the earth. God, however, has shown that robbing one's workers of a fair wage is just as sinful as robbing a bank. Voting for a racist because he is a racist is just as sinful as sleeping with your neighbour's wife! Silent participation in a company that pollutes the environment and thus imposes heavy costs on others is just as wrong as destroying one's own lungs with tobacco.

God reveals his displeasure at evil *institutions* very clearly in Amos 5:10-15. (To understand this passage, it is essential to remember that Israel's court sessions were held at the city gate.) "They hate him who reproves in the gate. ... I know how many are your transgressions, and how great are your sins—you who ... take a bribe, and turn aside the needy in the gate. ... Hate evil, and love good, and establish justice in the gate." "Let justice roll down like waters" (Amos 5:24) is not abstract verbalization. The prophet means justice in the legal system. He means: Get rid of the corrupt legal system that allows the wealthy to buy their way out of trouble but gives the poor long prison terms.

Nor is it only the dishonest and corrupt individuals in the legal system who stand condemned. God clearly revealed that laws themselves are sometimes an abomination to him.

> *Can wicked rulers be allied with thee,*
> *who frame mischief by statute?*
> *They band together against the life of the righteous,*
> *and condemn the innocent to death.*
> *But the LORD has become my stronghold,*
> *and my God the rock of my refuge.*
> *He will bring back on them their iniquity*
> *and wipe them out for their wickedness;*
> *the LORD our God will wipe them out. (Ps. 94:20-23)*

The Jerusalem Bible has an excellent rendition of verse 20: "You never consent to that corrupt tribunal that imposes disorder as law." God wants his people to know that wicked governments "frame mischief by statute". Or, as the New English Bible puts it, they contrive evil "under cover of law".

God proclaims the same word through the prophet Isaiah:

> *Woe to those who decree iniquitous decrees,*
> *and the writers who keep writing oppression,*
> *to turn aside the needy from justice*
> *and to rob the poor of my people of their right...*
> *What will you do on the day of punishment,*
> *in the storm which will come from afar?*
> *To whom will you flee for help,*
> *and where will you leave your wealth?*

> *Nothing remains but to crouch among the prisoners*
> *or fall among the slain.*
> *For all this his [God's] anger is not turned away*
> *and his hand is stretched out still. (Is. 10 :1–4)*

It is quite possible to make oppression legal. Then, as now, legislators devised unjust laws and the bureaucracy (the scribes or writers) implemented the injustice. But God shouts a divine woe against those rulers who use their official position to write unjust laws and unfair legal decisions. Legalized oppression is an abomination to our God. Therefore, he commands his people to avoid alliances (Ps. 94:20) with wicked governmental establishments that frame mischief by statute.

The just Lord of the universe will also destroy wicked rulers and unjust social institutions (see also 1 Kings 21). God cares about evil economic structures and unjust legal systems—precisely because they destroy people by the hundreds and thousands and millions.

There is another side to institutionalized evil which makes it especially pernicious. Structural evil is so subtle that one can be ensnared and hardly realize it. God inspired his prophet Amos to utter some of the harshest words in Scripture against the cultured, kind, upper-class ladies of his day:

Hear this word, you cows of Bashan . . . [you] who oppress the poor, who crush the needy, who say to [your] husbands, "Bring that we may drink!" The LORD God has sworn by his holiness that, behold, the days are coming upon you, when they shall take you away with hooks, even the last of you with fishhooks. (Amos 4:1–2)

The ladies involved may have had little direct contact with the impoverished peasants. They may never have realized clearly that their gorgeous clothes and spirited parties were possible only because of the sweat and tears of toiling peasants. In fact they may even have been kind on occasion to individual peasants they met. (Perhaps they gave them "Christmas baskets" once a year.) But God called these privileged women "cows" because they profited from social evil. Hence they were personally and individually guilty before God.[4]

If one is a member of a privileged class that profits from

structural evil and if one does nothing to try to change things, one stands guilty before God. Social evil is just as displeasing to God as personal evil. And it affects more people and is more subtle.

The prophets also disclosed how the God of justice responds to oppressive social structures. God cares so much about the poor that he will destroy social structures that tolerate and foster great poverty. Over and over again God declared that he would destroy the nation of Israel because of *both* its idolatry *and* its mistreatment of the poor.

The both/and is crucial. We dare not become so preoccupied with horizontal issues of social justice that we neglect vertical evils such as idolatry. Modern Christians seem to have an irrepressible urge to fall into one extreme or the other. But the Bible corrects our one-sidedness. God destroyed Israel and Judah because of both their idolatry and their social injustice.

The following selections from Amos could be duplicated from many other places in Scripture.

Because you trample upon the poor and take from him exactions of wheat, you have built houses of hewn stone, but you shall not dwell in them. (Amos 5:11) Woe to those who lie upon beds of ivory, and stretch themselves upon their couches, and eat lambs from the flock, . . . but are not grieved over the ruin of Joseph. Therefore they shall now be the first of those to go into exile. (Amos 6: 4, 6, 7)

Hear this, you who trample upon the needy, and bring the poor of the land to an end, saying, "When will the new moon be over, that we may sell grain? And the sabbath, that we may offer wheat for sale. . . . and deal deceitfully with false balances, that we may buy the poor for silver and the needy for a pair of sandals? (Amos 8:4–6)

Behold, the eyes of the Lord GOD are upon the sinful kingdom, and I will destroy it from the surface of the ground. (Amos 9:8)

Within a generation after the time of the prophet Amos, the northern kingdom of Israel was completely wiped out.

Probably the most powerful statement of God's work to destroy evil social structures is in the New Testament—in Mary's Magnificat! Mary glorified the Lord who "has put down the mighty from their thrones, and exalted those of low degree;

[who] has filled the hungry with good things, and the rich he has sent empty away" (Lk. 1:52–53). The Lord of history is at work pulling down sinful societies where wealthy classes live from the sweat, toil and grief of the poor.

INSTITUTIONALIZED EVIL TODAY What does this biblical teaching mean for affluent Westerners? Are we exploiting the poor of the world in the way the wealthy did in Amos's day?

The answer, I think, is yes. Stanley Mooneyham, president of World Vision International, speaks of "the stranglehold which the developed West has kept on the economic throats of the Third World." He believes that "the heart of the problems of poverty and hunger are human systems which ignore, mistreat and exploit man . . . If the hungry are to be fed, . . . some of the systems will require drastic adjustments while others will have to be scrapped altogether."[5] Together we must examine the evidence for this evaluation.

I cite this disturbing data not with sadistic enjoyment of an opportunity to flagellate the affluent, but rather with deep pain over the agony and anguish that torment the poor.

All developed countries are directly involved. So too are the wealthy elites in poor countries. Ancient social patterns, inherited values and cherished philosophical perspectives in developing countries also contribute in an important way to present poverty.[6] It would be naïve to simplify complex realities and isolate one scapegoat. But surely *our* first responsibility is to pluck the beam from our own eye. Our most desperate need is to understand and change what we are doing wrong. How then are we a part of sinful structures that contribute to world hunger? We will look at four areas: international trade; consumption of natural resources; food consumption and food imports; and profits on investments.

INTERNATIONAL TRADE First, and most important, the industrialized nations have carefully shaped the patterns of international trade for their own economic advantage. Of all money that moves from rich to poor nations 80 per cent comes from international trade. Only 20 per cent results from foreign aid and foreign private investment.[7] Hence favourable patterns of international trade are crucial to developing nations.

Unjust trade patterns between rich and poor nations date back to colonial times. Not all aspects of colonialism were harmful, of course. But the mother countries regularly ran their colonies with a sharp eye for their own economic advantage.[8] Britain's treatment of the textile industry in Bengal provides one illustration. When Britain first took control of this part of India, Bengal's textile industry was well advanced. But Britain promptly imposed a system of tariffs and duties that permitted British goods to enter India duty-free. Heavy import duties, on the other hand, prevented Bengali manufacturers from competing in the British market. As a result, Britain's textile industry flourished and India's stagnated.[9]

Tariffs and other import restrictions are still an essential part of today's unjust international economic order.[10] The Kennedy round of tariff negotiations in the 1960s lowered the tariffs on goods traded among the rich industrial nations by 50 per cent. But it did little to lower tariffs on goods from poorer countries. The relative situation of the poor countries actually grew worse.[11]

Developed countries charge very high tariffs on processed and manufactured goods from poor countries. The less manufacturing and processing done by the poor country, the lower the tariff. The reason is simple. Entrenched processing and manufacturing interests (both Trade Unions and management) want the developed countries to be able to buy cheap raw materials and profit from processing and manufacturing them here.[12]

In his recent text, *Economic Development*, Professor Theodore Morgan summarises the situation as follows:

The overall pattern is plain. Primary and simple products have low duties, though some have quotas. Simple manufactures have higher duties; and complex manufactures still higher. There are sharp obstacles to major cuts in tariff and non-tariff barriers because of the resistance of domestic businessmen, labour groups, and regions, which fear injury from increased imports.[13]

The result is to deprive poor countries of millions of extra jobs and billions of extra pounds from increased exports.

On textiles, which many developing countries such as India could supply cheaply to developed countries, the developed world has placed quota restrictions, and there is strong pressure for these quotas to be reduced still further to aid ailing domestic industries in the developed countries.

Many Third World economists also charge that the overall relationship between prices of primary products exported by them and the prices of manufactured products exported by developed nations is unjust. (Although changes are occurring, most exports of developing countries continue to be unmanufactured, unprocessed primary products.) They point out that the prices of primary products fluctuate widely, disrupting their economies.

Even more serious is the charge that for decades the prices of their primary products with the exception of crude oil since 1973 have been declining relative to the prices of manufactured products and other high technology items which poor countries must buy from developed nations.

The government of Tanzania reports that one tractor cost five tons of sisal in 1963. In 1970 the same tractor cost ten tons of sisal. In 1960 a rubber exporting country could purchase six tractors with twenty-five tons of rubber. In 1975 the same amount of rubber would only buy two tractors.[14]

There is general agreement that a serious decline in the relative prices of primary products exported by developing countries has occurred in the last twenty-five years despite the boom in commodity prices in 73-74. The rise in tea and coffee prices in 1977 did a little to restore their real purchasing power, but increased crop costs and lower yields have offset much of these gains.

Hans Singer, for years a highly respected economist at the United Nations, argues: "It is a matter of historical fact that ever since the seventies [the 1870s] the trend of prices has been heavily against sellers of food and raw materials and in favour of the sellers of manufactured articles. The statistics are open to doubt and to objection in detail, but the general story which they tell is unmistakable."[15] The violent fluctuation of prices of primary products exported by developing countries is very harmful to their economies, and makes planning almost impossible as they depend on these exports not just for revenue, but for vital foreign exchange with which to buy essential imported goods. Some countries are dependent on just one commodity for virtually all their exports such as Bangladesh on jute and Zambia on copper and this makes their economies very sensitive to the world price of that commodity.

We have looked briefly at several aspects of present international trade patterns which work to the disadvantage of the developing nations: high tariffs (especially on manufactured goods) imposed by developed nations, quotas demanded by rich countries, and wild fluctuation in prices of their commodity exports. What has been the response of the developing nations?

They have protested about these unjust patterns of international trade for decades. At the Bandung Afro-Asian Conference in 1955 and at the 1964 U.N. Conference on Trade and Development, developing countries urged the rich nations to design more just trade patterns. But the affluent turned a deaf ear.

The fantastic success of the oil cartel since 1973 has finally produced at least superficial change. Until 1973 the price of oil was little better than the price of other raw materials exported by the Third World. Then the Oil Producing and Exporting Countries (OPEC) used the fact that they controlled a very high per cent of all oil exports. By working together they were able to raise prices 400 per cent within a couple of years.

However this hit not only the oil hungry economies of the developed world but also many non-oil producing countries of the Third World. They could not find the extra foreign exchange for their essential oil and fertilizer imports, particularly as their grain imports were costing them three times as much as in 1971–72. The OPEC countries have stepped up their aid programme, but this has not offset the adverse effects that the oil price increase had on many developing countries.

The increase in oil prices made the trading relationship between oil exporting developing countries and developed countries much more just and was of enormous help to their development, particularly the low income OPEC countries such as Indonesia and Nigeria.

If what has happened to oil prices would also happen to

other products and commodities produced by the poor nations, many more countries could, if their leaders wished, feed their hungry people and make greater strides toward development.[16]

Important proposals for a New International Economic Order have resulted from this changed situation. A Declaration and Action Programme and a Charter of Economic Rights and Duties of States for the New International Economic Order were adopted at the U.N. in April and December 1974. There were several key proposals:[17]

1. Prices of primary products and raw materials. These prices, the developing nations insisted, should increase immediately. Furthermore, the prices of these products should be tied directly to the prices of manufactured products which the poor nations must import from rich nations.

A common fund should be set up, which would be used to finance buffer stocks of twenty or thirty key commodities so that wild fluctuations in commodity prices could be ironed out.

2. Tariffs and other barriers to trade. Developed countries should remove tariffs and other trade barriers to products from the developing nations.

3. National sovereignty over national resources. This includes the right to nationalise foreign holdings with fair compensation.

4. Foreign aid. Rich nations should increase both emergency food aid and grants for long-term development. The U.N. target of 0·7 per cent of GNP on official development assistance by the developed countries should be achieved (see Table 9, p. 44).

5. The developing world should increase its share of world manufactured goods output from about 10 per cent in 1975 to 25 per cent by the year 2000.

6. Debt should be re-scheduled for many developing countries and for the poorest it should be cancelled. (Many developing countries spend a large proportion of their current aid on meeting interest and capital repayment on previous "aid".)

7. There should be arrangements for the transfer of technology from developed to developing countries, other than through multi-national companies of which developing countries are understandably, in the light of some of their recent experiences, very suspicious.

8. International monetary arrangements. The poor nations demanded a larger role in the International Monetary Fund and other international monetary arrangements which affect trade and development. In order to promote trade and help countries with balance-of-payments problems, the International Monetary Fund created Special Drawing Rights (SDRs) worth about $3 billion per year. James P. Grant, President of the Overseas Development Council, shows how unequally assets were distributed: "Under the distribution formula that was established, however, three-quarters of these assets were made available virtually without cost to the rich countries, since these countries again set up the system and determined how SDRs would be allocated."[18]

The reaction of the affluent nations to the proposals for a New International Economic Order was initially cautious and sometimes even hostile.

At the fourth UNCTAD Conference, held in Nairobi in May 1976, the developing countries pressed their demands for a New International Economic Order, but this time they had a powerful ally—OPEC. The OPEC countries made it clear that failure to agree eventually on the Common Fund for commodities might lead them to set higher prices for their crude oil. In the end, even after all night bargaining, no final agreement was reached on the Common Fund, largely because of the opposition of the U.S.A., Germany and Japan, who wanted a free market in commodities. However there was agreement to meet again in early 77, after the elections in those three countries.

This meeting took place in Paris in Spring 77, and there was agreement to set up a much more limited version of the Common Fund than the developing countries originally wanted. How this will work out in practice, and whether it will help prevent the wild fluctuations in commodity prices and halt or reverse the decline of commodity prices relative to manufactured goods remain to be seen.

Present patterns of international trade are fundamentally unjust. In chapters seven to nine we shall examine proposals for change—in our personal lifestyles, the church and society at large. For the present, it is enough to see that current trade patterns make it impossible to live in the affluent West and not be involved in unjust social structures.[19]

CONSUMPTION OF NON-RENEWABLE RESOURCES

Unfortunately, international trade is not the only way that we are implicated in structural evil. The rich nations use a very unfair share of the earth's limited non-renewable resources.

Rich Countries Consumption of Non-Renewable Natural Resources 1974–76

	Col 1 U.S.	Col 2 U.K.	Col 3 West Germany	Col 4 Canada	Col 5 Australia New Zealand	Col 6 E.E.C. Scandinavia N. America Australasia	Col 7 Europe N. America U.S.S.R. Japan Australasia
% of World Population	5·4	1·4	1·5	0·6	0·4	13·4	27·6
% of annual World Consumption of Resource							
Petroleum	28·5	3·5	4·8	3·1	1·3	53·7	83·0
Natural Gas	47·4	3·0	3·1	3·9	0·5	65·0	92·1
Aluminium	32·8	3·4	6·5	2·5	1·4	57·0	90·2
Copper	21·2	5·7	8·6	2·8	1·4	52·8	89·1
Lead	22·3	6·0	5·8	1·4	1·9	51·7	86·0
Nickel	24·1	4·7	8·2	1·8	0·6	50·6	94·2
Tin	23·8	6·4	6·1	2·0	1·7	51·6	84·1
Zinc	18·5	4·3	6·1	2·6	2·0	45·7	85·6

Sources: World Metal Statistics published by World Bureau of Metal Statistics. BP Statistical review of the World Oil Industry – 1976

Table 10

Table 10 Col. 7 shows the enormous proportion of these eight non-renewable natural resources consumed by the developed nations of the world to sustain our affluent consumer society. 27·6 per cent of the world's population accounts for between

83 and 94 per cent of total world consumption and this is despite the fact that during the period 1974–76 the Western World was in its worst recession for over forty years! The country breakdown shows that this is not just because of the profligacy of the U.S. and Canada. For lead, copper and tin, the U.K. had a higher average per capita consumption than the U.S. during these three years, and the same is true for other metals for other rich countries. Only for petroleum, natural gas and aluminium is North America's per capita consumption substantially higher than other rich nations.

Table 10 column 6 shows that even within the group of developed nations, the nominally "Christian" nations of the E.E.C., Scandinavia, North America and Australasia with only 13·4 per cent of the world's population account for over half the world's total annual consumption of all but one of these resources, and this is without the help of Japan, U.S.S.R. and 200 million people in the "poorer" countries of Eastern and Southern Europe!

As we ravenously consume the more easily recoverable reserves of these resources, the new sources of supply to replace them are often much more expensive to recover, partly because of the more sophisticated technology needed, such as oil from the north slope of Alaska and under the North Sea, but high prices now justify the exploitation. The high price however puts these resources out of the reach of most of the developing countries, who do not have large exportable reserves of non-renewable natural resources, so that they find it difficult to afford even the meagre quantities they do need for their own development. Even the producer country may not reap the benefit of the high price, because the increased cost of production leaves little room for profit to the country after the transnational company, which is needed more than ever now because of the high technology involved, has taken its profit. The only time a developing country is able to make substantial gains from exploiting its non-renewable resources is when there are high prices relative to the cost of production and the only major example of this happening is oil from OPEC countries.

Our per capita energy consumption is another example of

Per Capita Energy Consumption—1974—1976

Country	Kilograms per person (Coal Equivalent)		
	1974	1975	1976
U.S.	11,333	10,999	11,554
Canada	9,739	9,822	9,950
Australia	6,229	6,249	6,657
West Germany	5,764	5,345	5,922
U.K.	5,366	5,299	5,268
U.S.S.R.	4,836	5,063	5,233
Japan	3,839	3,639	3,679
Mexico	1,221	1,207	1,227
Brazil	664	684	731
India	199	213	218
Pakistan	188	188	181
Kenya	160	157	152
Sierra Leone	126	112	112
Nigeria	94	87	94
Bangladesh	29	28	32
Ethiopia	36	28	27
Burundi	11	9	11

Source: U.N. Statistical Year Book 1977.

Table 11

the staggering imbalance in resource consumption (see Table 11).

Table 11 on energy usage illustrates our affluence. At the end of 1973 and beginning of 1974, while Europeans complained about lack of petrol for their private motoring and Americans grumbled over long lines at the gas pumps, Indian farmers waited in line for days for a small can of fuel to run their irrigation pumps. And when they returned home empty handed, they also turned back in despair to earlier, less productive types of farming. If we persist in using so much energy, we will certainly help push up the world price of oil, and oil based fertilizers. As a result, poor countries will not be able to afford even the small amounts they so badly need. The result: less food and more starvation.

If the supply of natural resources were unlimited and others could soon enjoy the same benefits, the situation would be different. But that is not the case. International development specialist Lester Brown confesses that "it has long been part of the conventional wisdom within the international development community that the two billion people living in the poor countries could not aspire to the lifestyle enjoyed by the average westerner because there was not enough iron ore, petroleum and protein in the world to provide it."[20] Senator Hubert Humphrey was right: "The question I believe is going to come down to whether Americans will be willing to cut down their own consumption to help these poor people."[21]

The question could equally well be asked: are Europeans or Australasians willing to cut their consumption to help the poor of the developing world? Once we realize that the supply of natural resources is limited so that the poor nations cannot ever hope to enjoy our standard of living, is it just to demand an ever-expanding economy and an ever more affluent lifestyle? E. F. Schumacher puts it bluntly:

It is obvious that the world cannot afford the U.S.A. Nor can it afford Western Europe or Japan. . . Think of it—one American drawing on resources that would sustain fifty Indians ! . . . The poor don't do much damage; the modest people don't do much damage. Virtually all the damage is done by, say, 15 per cent . . . The problem passengers on Spaceship Earth are the first-class passengers and no one else.[22]

Fertilizer illustrates Schumacher's point very well. In late 1973 a severe, worldwide fertilizer shortage arose. What did the United States do? It quietly imposed a fertilizer embargo. In October 1973 (while protesting the Arab oil embargo), the U.S. government agreed with the fertilizer industry that all fertilizer export sales would be halted until June 1974. In terms of total global grain production, this was unwise. Since the U.S. already uses so much fertilizer, additional amounts applied in the United States do not produce as large an additional yield as the same amount would elsewhere. One additional ton of fertilizer produces ten more tons of grain in, say, India. In the U.S., it produces only five more tons of grain.[23]

Nor is that all. Americans use as much fertilizer on their lawns, gardens and golf-courses (3 million tons) as India uses for *all* purposes.[24] Because of the export restrictions on fertilizer, India had a serious shortfall of fertilizer in 1974. Partly because of this shortfall, cereal production in India fell from 118·4 million tons in 1973 to 108·2 million tons in 1974.[25] Put another way, per capita cereal production fell from 200 kg to 180 kg, although the population grew by less than 2 per cent.

It is simply incorrect to think that the population explosion in the poor countries is the sole or perhaps even the primary cause of widespread hunger in the world. Our ever-increasing affluence is also at the heart of the problem.

FOOD CONSUMPTION PATTERNS Our eating patterns—a third area where we are caught in institutionalized sin—may at first glance seem very personal and private. But they are tightly interlocked with complex economic structures including national and international agricultural policies and decisions of multinational corporations engaged in agribusiness.

The rich nations import far more food from poor nations than they export to them! Poor developing nations are feeding the affluent minority! I was astounded at the extent of net food imports from poor nations to rich nations when I first examined the data. Table 12 shows that from 1955 to 1973 the rich, developed nations imported approximately twice as many dollars worth of food from the poor, developing nations as they exported to them.

Western Europe and Japan account for a large percentage of these food imports from developing nations.

The division of the world fish catch is equally lopsided. If the 1973 world fish catch of 65·7 million tons had been divided evenly, each person in the world would have received thirty-four

Food Exports and Imports (millions of U.S. dollars)

	food exports from developed world to developing world		food imports by developed countries from developing		net *loss* of food by poor countries
year	all developed countries	Western Europe	all developed countries	Western Europe	(col. 4 minus col. 2)
Col. 1	Col. 2	Col. 3	Col. 4	Col. 5	Col. 6
1955	2090	965	6870	3830	4780
1960	3150	1210	7160	4190	4010
1961	3180	1200	6800	4000	3620
1962	3140	1090	7180	4360	4040
1963	3370	1100	8070	4900	4700
1964	3820	1200	8420	5060	4600
1965	3780	1250	8410	5110	4630
1966	4184	1265	8555	5030	4371
1967	4423	1369	8555	4995	4132
1968	4283	1420	9005	5010	4722
1969	4321	1528	9410	5375	5089
1970	5065	1688	10,680	6060	5615
1971	5710	1915	10,815	5805	5105
1972	6255	2240	12,770	7220	6515
1973	9805	3245	17,010	10,000	7205

Note: Communist countries are not included. Items included are: SITC 0, 1, 22, 4.
Source: U.N.'s *Handbook of International Trade and Development Statistics*, 1972 and U.N.'s *Monthly Bulletin of Statistics*, July, 1975 and Feb., 1976.

Table 12

pounds.[26] But it was not so divided! The rich nations (one-quarter of the world's people) demand three-quarters of the total world catch of fish each year. Japan, with a mere 3 per cent of the world's people, receives 20 per cent of the world fish catch.[27] Peru has the largest anchovy fisheries in the world. But not enough of the anchovy protein goes to feed the millions of poor Peruvians.[28] Instead, most of it fattens livestock in Europe and the United States.

Professor Georg Borgstrom has summarized the situation for us:

Through oilseeds, oilseed products, and fish meal, the Western World is currently acquiring from the Hungry World one million metric tons more protein than is delivered to the Hungry World through grains. In other words, the Western World is exchanging approximately 3 million metric tons of cereal protein for 4 million metric tons of other proteins which are all superior in a nutritive respect. This flow from the Hungry World is depriving millions in tropical Africa, Latin America, and Asia of their major deficit commodity. The Satisfied World is thus taking no small amount of protein from the world's scarce supplies.[29]

The rich minority maintain their affluent eating patterns by net imports from lands where millions are starving.

"But surely North America is different!" Yes, to some extent. Canada and the United States remain among the very few net exporters of food to the world as a whole.

But this looks startlingly different when U.S. food imports and exports to poor, developing nations are compared. Every year from 1955 to 1972, the United States imported more food from poor nations than it exported to hungry lands!

The statistics of Table 13 shocked me. I could hardly believe at first that the United States had regularly taken more food from hungry nations than it has returned. But the statistics are clear. In 1972 developing nations sent the U.S. $1·5 billion worth of food more than was sent to them. "The United States alone imports about twice as much fish, primarily in the form of feed for livestock, as *do all the poor countries combined*"[30] (my emphasis). Two-thirds of the total world catch of tuna comes to the United States. One-third of the tuna imported to the United States goes for catfood![31]

It is not simply that North Americans consume five times as much grain as do most Asians. It is not simply that each day they eat twice as much protein as their bodies need. It is not simply that they devour so many unnecessary calories that more

U.S. Food Imports from and Exports to Developing Countries (millions of U.S. dollars)

year	U.S. food exports to developing countries	U.S. food exports to developed countries	U.S. food imports from developing countries	net *loss* by poor countries
1955	735	1800	2470	1735
1960	1470	2230	2450	980
1961	1460	2550	2270	810
1962	1570	2780	2300	730
1963	1750	3050	2400	650
1964	2000	3320	2540	540
1965	1900	3700	2520	620
1966	2171	4100	2685	514
1967	2167	3630	2755	588
1968	2094	3545	3096	1002
1969	1876	3690	2982	1106
1970	2160	4555	3425	1265
1971	2250	4670	3656	1406
1972	2580	5545	4027	1447

Note: Communist countries are not included. Items included: SITC 0, 1, 22, 4.

Source: U.N.'s *Handbook of International Trade and Development Statistics*, 1972, and the U.N.'s *Monthly Bulletin of Statistics*, July, 1975, and Feb., 1976.

Table 13

than 80 million of them are overweight. They can do all these foolish, unjust things, in part because each year the poor world exports vast quantities of food to the U.S.!

Cowboys and beef cattle are part of America's national self-identity. Surely their beef at least is all grown at home? By no means! The United States is the world's largest importer of beef![32] Imported beef comes not just from Australia and New Zealand, but also from many countries in Latin America. "The

Mexican border," Professor Borgstrom points out, "is the scene of the world's biggest meat transfers."[33] Americans import approximately one million cattle every year from Mexico. In fact Americans import half as much Mexican beef as all Mexicans have left for themselves.[34]

Again it is not merely that they consume beef that hungry Mexicans need. Their demand for beef also encourages unjust structures in Mexico. Mexico's economy has been growing at the exceptionally high annual rate of 6–7 per cent for the last fifteen years. But unemployment and the income differential between rich and poor have also spurted forward. Why? Because the government has stressed large farms and urban factories rather than a pattern of development that would benefit everyone. Almost all of the increasing farm production has come from fewer than 5 per cent of the farms. This small fraction of all Mexican farms employs a mere one-sixth of all farm labourers.[35] As a result, 20 per cent of all Mexicans receive 64 per cent of the total income while 40 per cent of the people get a mere 10 per cent![36] The result is unemployment and hunger especially in the countryside. Mexico might have decided to adopt a different development strategy (using people rather than machines) that would have provided food for the masses rather than beef for export. But U.S. desire for beef encouraged a different pattern.

There are many other examples. Honduras is a poor Central American country where one-third of the people earn less than thirty dollars a year.[37] In spite of widespread poverty they export large amounts of beef to the United States. The United States recently raised the beef import quota of Honduras from 27·8 to 34·8 million pounds. Beef for export is grown largely by a tiny wealthy elite of 667 families (0·3 per cent of the total population) who own 27·4 per cent of all cultivable land.[38]

Right now an intense struggle rages in Honduras. The poor peasants want more land. Predictably, the powerful Honduran Cattle Farmers' Federation, which represents the wealthy farmers, objects. A group of cattle farmers recently attacked a peasant training centre, killing several people. The wealthy farmers want to continue growing beef for Americans. Earlier it was mentioned that a study on Latin America had shown that malnutrition was either the primary cause or a major contributory factor in more than half of the deaths of children under five in Latin American countries.[39] Who is responsible for those dying children? The wealthy Hondurans who want to protect their affluence? The American companies that work closely with the Honduran elite? The Americans who eat the beef needed by hundreds of thousands of hungry children in Honduras?

We dare not, of course, make the simplistic assumption that if we merely stop eating beef, hungry Mexicans and Hondurans will promptly enjoy it. Complex economic and political changes are required. Chapter nine examines some of the ways we can promote such changes. My purpose here is to show that our eating patterns are interlocked with destructive social and economic structures that leave millions hungry and starving.

PROFITS ON INVESTMENTS In the spring of 1975, while waiting for a bus at the Philadelphia airport, I began a casual conversation with a fellow traveller. He was a businessman who had spent most of his life in Latin America. He seemed eager to share his annoyance and surprise at the rapidly growing anti-American sentiment in Latin America. Since he had spent a lot of time working for U.S.-owned and -related companies in Venezuela, I asked what profit we had made on our investments there. After a second's pause, he replied: "Probably two hundred times what we invested." And he was still puzzled by growing anti-Americanism!

He undoubtedly overestimated the return even for Venezuela. Certainly it has not been that great in the rest of the continent. But even when the risk factor is considered, profits have been high. In 1971 the U.S. Department of Commerce reported that "the rate of return [for 1970] on investments in less developed countries was 21 per cent, roughly twice the yield on investments in the developed areas."[40]

Large profits on capital invested in poor countries return to the United States every year. In 1973 U.S. direct investments abroad amounted to $107 billion. About one-fourth of that ($28 billion) was invested in poor countries. But one-third of the total $17·5 billion in profits on those foreign investments came from poor countries.[41]

These investments give the United States powerful influence in other countries, especially Latin America. Gunnar Myrdal estimates that "United States corporations now control or decisively influence between 70 and 90 per cent of the raw-materials resources of Latin America, and probably much more than half of its modern manufacturing, industry, banking, commerce, and foreign trade."[42] The result is a large annual transfer of cash from a relatively poor continent to a rich one. Republican Senator Charles McC. Mathias, Jr. of Maryland has said that "capital flows *from* Latin America and *into* the United States are now over four times as great as the flow south. The countries of Latin America, in a way, are actually giving foreign aid to the United States, the wealthiest country in the world."[43]

Former Chilean President Allende used high profits as an explanation for his expropriation of copper mines owned by U.S. firms. (The CIA subsequently used millions of U.S. tax dollars to help overthrow his democratically elected government.) Allende pointed out that there were 700,000 children in Chile who were physically and mentally retarded for life because they had not received adequate protein. While these children were growing into stunted adulthood, U.S. copper companies were sending high profits out of the country. These profits could have filled the protein deficit for decades if they had been available for the poor Chileans rather than affluent U.S. investors.[44]

We are all implicated in structural evil. International trade patterns are unjust. An affluent minority devours most of the earth's non-renewable natural resources. Food consumption patterns are grossly lopsided. And the returns on investments in poor countries are unjustly high. Every person in developed countries benefits from these structural injustices. Unless you have retreated to some isolated valley and grow or make everything you use, you participate in unjust structures which contribute directly to the hunger of a billion malnourished neighbours.

The conclusion of course is not that international trade or

investment in poor countries is always immoral. Nor is it that the economies of the developed world would be destroyed if these injustices were corrected. The proper conclusion is that injustice has become embedded in some of our fundamental economic institutions. Biblical Christians—precisely to the extent that they are faithful to Scripture—will dare to call such structures sinful.

The reader without a degree in economics probably wishes international economics were less complex or that faithful discipleship in our time had less to do with such a complicated subject. But former U.N. Secretary General, Dag Hammar-skjöld, was right: "In our era, the road to holiness necessarily passes through the world of action."[45] To give the cup of cold water effectively in the Age of Hunger frequently requires some understanding of international economic and political structures. The story of bananas helps clarify these complex issues.

THE STORY OF BANANAS On April 10, 1975, North Americans learned that United Brands, one of three huge U.S. companies that grow and import bananas, had arranged to pay $2·5 million (only $1·25 million was actually paid) in bribes to top government officials in Honduras. Why? To persuade them to impose an export tax on bananas that was less than half of what Honduras had requested![46] In order to increase profits for a U.S. company and to lower banana prices, the Honduran govenment agreed, for a bribe, to cut drastically the export tax, even though the money was desperately needed in Honduras.

The story actually began in March 1974. Several banana producing countries in Central America agreed to join together to demand a $1·00 tax on every case of bananas exported. Why? Banana prices for producers had not increased in the last twenty inflation-ridden years. But the costs for manufactured goods had constantly escalated. As a result the real purchasing power of exported bananas had declined by 60 per cent. At least half of the export income in countries like Honduras and Panama comes from bananas. No wonder they are poor. (As we have already seen, one-third of the inhabitants of Honduras earn less than thirty dollars a year!)

What did the banana companies do when the exporting countries demanded a one dollar tax on bananas? They adamantly refused to pay. Since three large companies (United Brands, Castle and Cooke, and Del Monte) control ninety percent of the marketing and distribution of bananas, they had powerful leverage. In Panama the fruit company abruptly stopped cutting bananas. In Honduras the banana company allowed 145,000 crates to rot at the docks. One after another the poor countries gave in. Costa Rica finally settled for twenty-five cents a crate. Panama, for thirty-five cents. Honduras, thanks to the large bribe, eventually agreed to a thirty cent tax.[47]

One can easily understand why a U.N. fact-finding commission in 1975 concluded, "The banana-producing countries with very much less income are subsidizing the consumption of the fruit, and consequently the development of the more industrialized countries."[48]

Why don't the masses of poor people demand change? They do. But they have little power. Dictators representing a tiny, wealthy elite that works closely with American business interests rule Honduras and many other Latin American countries.

The history of Guatemala, a neighbour of Honduras and also a producer of bananas for United Brands, shows why change is difficult. In 1954 the CIA helped overthrow a democratically-elected government in Guatemala. Why? Because it had initiated a modest programme of agricultural reform that seemed to threaten unused land owned by the United Fruit Company (the former name of United Brands). The U.S. Secretary of State in 1954 was John Foster Dulles. His law firm had written the company's agreements with Guatemala in 1930 and 1936. The CIA Director was Allen Dulles (brother of John Foster Dulles) who had been president of United Fruit Company. The Assistant Secretary of State was a major shareholder in United Fruit Company.[49] In Guatemala and elsewhere change is difficult because U.S. companies work closely with wealthy, local elites to protect their mutual economic interests.

Why are bananas in North American and European supermarkets so inexpensive? Surely each of us profits, often unconsciously, from very unjust patterns of international trade.

Tragically there will always be those eager to provide plausible rationalizations. Andrew M. Greeley, a prominent American sociologist at the University of Chicago, recently mocked those who try to make Americans "feel guilty" about their economic relationships with the Third World:

Well, let us suppose that our guilt finally becomes too much to bear and we decide to reform . . . We inform the fruit orchards in Central America that we can dispense with bananas in our diets . . . Their joy will hardly be noticed as massive unemployment and depression sweep those countries.[50]

One wonders if Greeley is naïve or perverse. The point is not—and Greeley surely knows this—that we should stop importing bananas. Rather, it is that we should pay fair prices and promote programmes here and in Central America that will help people in the producing countries enjoy a decent life.

The example of bananas shows how all of us are involved in very unjust international economic structures. The words of the apostle James seem to speak directly to our situation.

Come now, you rich, weep and howl for the miseries that are coming upon you . . . Your gold and silver have rusted, and their rust will be evidence against you . . . Behold, the wages of the labourers who mowed your fields, which you kept back by fraud, cry out; and the cries of the harvesters have reached the ears of the Lord of Hosts. You have lived on the earth in luxury and in pleasure; you have fattened your hearts in a day of slaughter. (James 5:1–5)

THE REPENTANCE OF ZACCHAEUS What should be our response, brothers and sisters? For biblical Christians the only possible response to sin is repentance. Unconsciously, at least to a degree, we have become entangled in a complex web of institutionalized sin. Thank God we can repent. God is merciful. He forgives. But only if we repent. And biblical repentance involves more than a hasty tear and a weekly prayer of confession. Biblical repentance involves conversion. It involves a whole new lifestyle. The One who stands ready to forgive us for our sinful involvement in terrible economic injustice offers us his grace to begin living a radically new lifestyle of identification with the poor and oppressed.

Sin is not just an inconvenience or a tragedy for our neighbours. It is a damnable outrage against the Almighty Lord of the universe. If God's Word is true, then all of us who dwell in affluent nations are trapped in sin. We have profited from systemic injustice—sometimes only half knowing, sometimes only half caring and always half hoping not to know. We are guilty of an outrageous offence against God and neighbour.

But that is not God's last word to us. If it were, honest acknowledgment of our involvement would be almost impossible. If there were no hope of forgiveness, admission of our sinful complicity in evil of this magnitude would be an act of despair.[51] But there is hope. The One who writes our indictment is the One who died for us sinners.

John Newton was captain of a slave ship in the eighteenth century. A brutal, callous man, he played a central role in a horrendous system which fed tens of thousands to the sharks and delivered millions to a living death. But one day he saw his sin and repented. His familiar hymn overflows with joy and gratitude for God's acceptance and forgiveness.

> *Amazing grace! How sweet the sound,*
> *that saved a wretch like me;*
> *I once was lost, but now am found,*
> *was blind but now I see.*
> *'Twas grace that taught my heart to fear,*
> *and grace my fears relieved;*
> *How precious did that grace appear*
> *the hour I first believed.*

John Newton became a founder member of the society for the abolition of slavery. The church of which he was pastor, St. Mary Woolnoth in the City of London, was a meeting place for abolitionists. William Wilberforce frequently came to him for spiritual counsel. Newton became famous for his impassioned sermons against the slave trade and these convinced many people of its evil. He campaigned against the slave trade until he died in the year of its abolition, 1807.

We are participants in a system that dooms even more people to agony and death. If we have eyes to see, God's grace will also teach our hearts to fear and tremble, and then also to rest and trust.

But only if we repent. Repentance is not coming forward at

the close of a service. It is not repeating a spiritual law. It is not mumbling a liturgical confession. All of those things may help. But they are no substitute for the kind of deep inner anguish that leads to a new way of living.

Biblical repentance entails conversion. Literally the word means "turning around". The Greek word *metanoia*, as Luther insisted so vigorously, means a total change of mind. The New Testament links repentance to a transformed style of living. Sensing the hypocrisy of the Pharisees who came seeking baptism, John the Baptist denounced them as a brood of vipers. "Bear fruit that befits repentance," he demanded (Mt. 3:8). Wherever he preached, Paul informed King Agrippa, he called on people to "repent and turn to God and perform deeds worthy of repentance" (Acts 26:20).

Zacchaeus should be our model. As a greedy Roman tax collector, Zacchaeus was enmeshed in sinful economic structures. But he never supposed that he could come to Jesus and still continue enjoying all the economic benefits of that systemic evil. Coming to Jesus meant repenting of his complicity in social injustice. It meant publicly giving reparations. And it meant a whole new lifestyle.

What might genuine, biblical repentance mean for affluent Christians entangled in their society's sinful structures? Part three examines this question.

PART III

IMPLEMENTATION

Where should we change?

A prominent Washington think-tank recently assembled a large cross-section of distinguished religious leaders to discuss the problems of world hunger. The conferees expressed deep concern. They called for significant structural change. But their words rang hollow. They were meeting at a very expensive, exclusive resort in Colorado! Simpler personal life-styles are essential.

But personal change is insufficient. I have a friend who has forsaken the city for a rural community. He grows almost all his own food, lives very simply and places very few demands on the poor of the earth. Unfortunately this person has considerable speaking and writing talents which could promote change in church and society, but he is failing to use them to the full.

We need to change at three levels. Simple personal life-styles are crucial to symbolize, validate and facilitate our concern for the hungry. The church must change so that its common life presents a new model for a divided world. Finally, the structures of secular society, both here and abroad, require revision.

TOWARD A SIMPLER LIFESTYLE

BEFORE GOD AND A BILLION HUNGRY NEIGHBOURS, WE MUST RETHINK OUR VALUES REGARDING OUR PRESENT STANDARD OF LIVING AND PROMOTE MORE JUST ACQUISITION AND DISTRIBUTION OF THE WORLD'S RESOURCES. [THE CHICAGO DECLARATION OF EVANGELICAL SOCIAL CONCERN (1973)[1]]

THOSE OF US WHO LIVE IN AFFLUENT CIRCUMSTANCES ACCEPT OUR DUTY TO DEVELOP A SIMPLE LIFESTYLE IN ORDER TO CONTRIBUTE MORE GENEROUSLY TO BOTH RELIEF AND EVANGELISM. [LAUSANNE COVENANT (1974)[2]]

THE RICH MUST LIVE MORE SIMPLY THAT THE POOR MAY SIMPLY LIVE. [DR. CHARLES BIRCH (1975)[3]]

We affluent Westerners have a problem. We actually believe that we can just barely get along on the three, four or five thousand pounds that we make. We are in an incredible rat race. When our net income goes up by another £100 in real terms we convince ourselves that we *need* about that much more to live —comfortably.

How can we escape this delusion? How will we respond to the desperate plight of the world's poor? Ten thousand persons died today because of inadequate food. One billion people are malnourished. The problem, we know, is that the world's resources are not evenly distributed. We in the developed world live on an affluent island amid a sea of starving humanity.

How will we respond to this gross inequality?

But how much should we give? Should we congratulate the Christian millionaire who tithes faithfully?

John Wesley gave a startling answer. One of his frequently repeated sermons was on Mt. 6:19-23 ("Lay not up for yourselves treasures upon earth . . .")[4] Christians should give away all but "the plain necessaries of life"—that is, plain, wholesome food, clean clothes and enough to carry on one's business. One should earn what one can, justly and honestly. But all income should be given to the poor after one satisfies bare necessities. Unfortunately, Wesley discovered there is not one person in five hundred in any "Christian city" who obeys Jesus' command. But that simply demonstrates that most professed believers are "living men but dead Christians". Any "Christian" who takes for himself anything more than the "plain necessaries of life", Wesley insisted, "lives in an open, habitual denial of the Lord." He has "gained riches and hell-fire!"[5]

Wesley lived what he preached. Sales of his books often earned him £1,400 annually, but he spent only £28 on himself. The rest he gave away. He always wore inexpensive clothes and dined on simple food. "If I leave behind me ten pounds," he once wrote, "you and all mankind bear witness against me that I lived and died a thief and a robber."[6,7]

Wesley's practice reflects biblical principles. In chapter four we discussed the biblical command for the year of Jubilee and Paul's collection for the impoverished Jerusalem church. We saw that God disapproves of great extremes of wealth and poverty. How much should we give? We should give until our lives truly reflect the principles of Leviticus 25 and 2 Corinthians 8. Surely Paul's advice to the Corinthians applies even more forcefully to Christians today in the Northern Hemisphere: "I do not mean that others should be eased and you burdened, but that *as a matter of equality* your abundance at the present time should supply their want . . . . *that there may be equality*" (2 Cor. 8:13-14, my emphasis).

THE GOD OF THE AFFLUENT WEST AND ITS PROPHET Why are we so unconcerned, so slow to care? One reason becomes apparent from the story of the rich young ruler. When he asked Jesus how to obtain eternal life, Jesus told him to sell all his goods and give to the poor. But the man went away sad because he had great possessions. Now as we are usually told, the point of the story undoubtedly is that if we want to follow Christ, he alone must be at the centre of our affections and plans. Whether the idol be riches, fame, status, academic distinction or membership of any in-group, we must be willing to abandon it for Christ's sake. Riches just happened to be this young man's idol. Jesus then is not commanding us to sell all our possessions, he is demanding total submission to himself.

This interpretation is both unquestionably true and unquestionably inadequate. To say no more is to miss the fact that wealth and possessions are the most common idols of us rich Westerners. Jesus, I suspect, meant it when he added, "Truly, I say to you, it will be hard for a rich man [especially for the twentieth-century Westerner] to enter the kingdom of heaven. Again I tell you, it is easier for a camel to go through the eye of a needle than for a rich man to enter the kingdom of God" (Mt. 19:23–24).

We have become ensnared by unprecedented material luxury. Advertising constantly convinces us that we really need one unnecessary luxury after another. The standard of living is the god of the twentieth-century Westerner, and the ad man is its prophet.

We all know how subtle the materialistic temptations are and how convincing the rationalizations. Only by God's grace and with great effort can we escape the shower of luxuries which has almost suffocated our Christian compassion. All of us face this problem. A couple of years ago, I spent about fifty dollars on an extra suit. That's not much of course. Besides, I persuaded myself that it was a wise investment (thanks to the 75 per cent reduction). But that money would have fed a starving child in India for about a year. In all honesty we have to ask ourselves: Dare we care at all about current fashions if that means reducing our ability to help hungry neighbours? Dare we care more about obtaining a secure economic future for our family than for living an uncompromisingly Christian lifestyle?

I do not pretend that giving an honest answer to such questions will be easy. Our responsibility is not always clear. One Saturday morning as I was beginning to prepare a lecture (on poverty!), a poor man came into my office and asked for five dollars. He was drinking. He had no food, no job, no home. The Christ of the poor confronted me in this man. But I didn't have the time, I said. I had to prepare a lecture on the Christian view of poverty. To be sure I did give him a couple of dollars, but that was not what he needed. He needed somebody to talk to, somebody to love him. He needed my time. He needed me. But I was too busy. "Inasmuch as you did it not to the least of these, you did it not . . ."

We Christians need to make some dramatic, concrete moves to escape the materialism that seeps into our minds via the diabolically clever and incessant radio and TV commercials. We have been brainwashed to believe that bigger houses, more prosperous businesses and more luxurious gadgets are worthy goals in life. As a result, we are caught in an absurd, materialistic spiral. The more we make, the more we think we need in order to live decently and respectably. Somehow we have to break this cycle because it makes us sin against our needy brothers and sisters and, therefore, against our Lord.

THE GRADUATED TITHE The graduated tithe is one of many models which can help break this materialistic stranglehold. I share it because it has proved helpful in our family. Obviously it is not the only useful model. Certainly it is not a biblical norm to be prescribed legalistically for others. We are very aware of the fact that it is only a modest beginning.

When Arbutus and I decided to adopt a graduated scale for our giving in 1969, we started by sitting down and trying to calculate honestly what we would need to live for a year. We wanted a figure that would permit reasonable comfort but not all the luxuries. I suspect that we arrived at this base amount somewhat arbitrarily. The authors of *Limits to Growth* suggest a standard of living which everyone in the world could share without rapidly depleting our natural resources and provoking prompt ecological disaster.[8] Perhaps their figure of $1800 per adult per year might offer a more rational way to arrive at one's base amount.

Somehow we arrived at a figure of $7,000. (Two growing boys and a new daughter have recently raised it to $8,000.) We decided to continue giving a tithe of 10 per cent on this basic amount. Then for every additional thousand dollars of income above that basic amount, we decide to increase our giving by 5 per cent on that thousand. Table 14 shows how it works out for an income of $13,000 and a base amount of $8,000.

Income	kingdom giving percentage	kingdom giving amount
First $8,000	10%	$800
Next 1000	15%	150
Next 1000	20%	200
Next 1000	25%	250
Next 1000	30%	300
Next 1000	35%	350
Total $13,000		$2,050

Table 14

Trying to compare U.S. incomes with incomes in the U.K. is difficult, but a figure of $3 to a £1 might give a more accurate purchasing power equivalence, since most goods and services in the U.S. are more expensive than in the U.K. if the official parity of $1·95 = £1 (Jan 1978) is used. (Petrol is one of the few goods that is actually cheaper in the U.S.)

The following suggestions may help those who want to develop their own version of the graduated tithe. First, discuss the idea with the whole family. Everyone needs to understand the reasons so that the family can come to a common decision. Second, spell out your plan in writing at the beginning of the

153

year. It is relatively painless, in fact exciting, to work it out theoretically. After you commit yourself to the abstract figures, it hurts less to dole out the cash each month! Third, discuss your proposal with a committed Christian friend or couple who share your concern for justice. Fourth, discuss major expenditures with the same people. It is easier for a slightly more objective observer to spot rationalizations than it is for you. (They also may have helpful hints on simple living.) Five, each year try to reduce your basic figure *and total expenditures*. (One suggestion for doing this: When you alter your figures because of inflation each year, do not alter them by the full amount.) The ultimate goal should be to reduce total expenditures (rather than the basic figure on which one pays a tithe of 10 per cent) to the point where you enjoy a standard of living which all persons in the world could share.

As the perceptive reader has already noticed, this proposal for a graduated tithe is really an extremely modest one. In fact the proposal is probably so modest that it verges on unfaithfulness to Saint Paul. But it is also sufficiently radical that its implementation would revolutionize the ministry and life of the church! Many Christians are experimenting with far more radical attempts to win the war on affluence.

A LIBERATED FAMILY   A few years ago Ginny and Walt Hearn were typical, successful professionals. Ginny had formerly been associate editor of Inter-Varsity Christian Fellowship's *HIS* magazine. Walt was a biochemistry professor at Iowa State University. But the professional rat race left little time to think, write or enjoy their two children. So they decided to adopt a much simpler lifestyle.

Walt and Ginny cut their spending in half, and put half their income in a savings account. After two years, they were ready for a dramatic change. They quit their jobs! Then they moved to Berkeley, bought an old house, and began to learn how to live on a fraction of their former income. How do they manage?

We stay out of stores as much as possible. We go to Salvation Army outlets for most of our clothes, to day-old bakery shops, to supermarkets for sale items, to flea markets—but shop prudently at them all. Secondhand bargains may come from classified ads, co-op bulletin boards, or garage sales. For books we first try libraries, then second-hand book-stores.

Our home menu features many "clean-out-the-icebox" soups, each as unique as you will find in a quaint foreign restaurant. Bones for our soup stock are more often cheap chicken backs than beef or pork.

Taking care of the possessions we have has more appeal than buying new ones. "Making do" is the educational side of doing without. Clothes, shoes, appliances, tools, almost anything can be kept in use with glue, patches, tape, "baling wire," and ingenuity.

We've become alert scavengers in vacant lots and junk piles, delighting to find some use for what other people discard. Our waffle iron came from a garbage can, but it works. Foraging has supplied berries, nuts, fruit, and fireplace wood that otherwise would have gone to waste. Having a VW makes scrounging easier and shopping cheaper, but we try not to "run around". Instead we plan trips to include several errands in one vicinity. We walk as much as we can for economy, health and ecology, and often take a bus instead of driving our car.

Since "entertainment" is such an expensive luxury, it is worth scanning the newspaper for low-cost movies, plays, and musical events. And there are museums and parks to explore. Simple pleasures like reading, walking, talking with friends, playing tennis, inviting people home for a meal, are more rewarding than most activities you have to pay for.[9]

The Hearns' simple lifestyle leaves plenty of time for important volunteer work. They have taught a (free) course on "Simple Living" at a "Free University" run by Christians in Berkeley. They devote a great deal of time to the Berkeley Christian Coalition, an evangelical group involved in evangelism, social action and the publication of *Radix*.

Walt and Ginny have survived the dramatic transition and love the change! They have time now for the writing that never got done before. And they are beginning to earn a very modest income from writing. But they will never return to affluent living. "Whenever we do begin to earn more money, we are resolved not to let our 'standard of living' rise along with our income. We are beginning to feel liberated."[10]

LIVING IN COMMUNITY   The model which permits the simplest standard of living is probably living in community. Housing, furniture, appliances, tools and car that would normally serve one nuclear family can accommodate ten or twenty people. Communal living releases vast amounts of money and people-time for alternative activities.

Many Christian communes have been initiated as conscious attempts to develop a more ecologically responsible and less unjust standard of living. But not all are so deliberate. The Church of the Redeemer in Houston, Texas, is interesting because its simple communal lifestyle "just happened." This inner-city, Episcopal church was virtually dead fifteen years ago. Then a charismatic renewal occurred. Scores of needy persons requiring special love and nurture flocked to Redeemer. Communal living seemed the only answer.

By 1976 about three hundred and fifty people lived communally in approximately thirty-five different households. Each household has eight to fifteen members. In a typical household of say eleven persons, two are wage-earners working at outside jobs. The rest are available to staff the numerous programmes of the church.

Of the income of each household, 20 per cent goes to the church. The remainder permits a modest lifestyle for the members. Jerry Barker explains how their simple lifestyle emerged. *It soon became obvious that the needs we were faced with would take lots of resources and so we began to cut expenses for things we had been accustomed to. We stopped buying new cars and new televisions and things of that sort. We didn't even think of them. We started driving our cars until they literally fell apart and then we'd buy a used car or something like that to replace it. We began to turn in some of our insurance policies so that they would not be such a financial drain on us. We found such security in our relationship with the Lord that it was no longer important to have security for the future . . . We never have had any rule about it, or felt this was a necessary part of the Christian life. It was just a matter of using the money we had available most effectively, particularly in supporting so many extra people. We learned to live very economically. We quit eating steaks and expensive roasts and things like that and we began to eat simple fare . . .* [11]

The standard of living of Christian communities varies. But almost all live far more simply than the average North American family. At Chicago's Reba Place, for example (see chapter eight), eating patterns are based on the welfare level of the city. Christian communes have a symbolic importance today out of all proportion to their numbers. They quietly question this society's affluence. And they offer a viable alternative.

Biblical Christians are experimenting with a variety of simple lifestyles today. An Age of Hunger demands drastic change. But we must be extremely careful to avoid legalism and self-righteousness. No one model is God's will for everyone. You are not necessarily more righteous if you live on $2,000 less per year than a Christian friend. Walt and Ginny Hearn have put it well: "We have to beware of the reverse snobbery of spiritual one-up-manship. . . We don't want to over-generalize from our experience; God seems to love variety."[12]

PRACTICAL SUGGESTIONS The following are hints, not rules. Freedom, joy and laughter are essential elements of simple living.

1. Reduce your food budget by:

☐ gardening: try hoeing instead of mowing; how about getting an allotment?

☐ substituting vegetable protein for animal protein.

☐ fasting regularly; It is biblical!

☐ setting a monthly budget and sticking to it.

2. Question your own lifestyle, not your neighbours'.

3. Lower energy consumption by:

☐ keeping your thermostat (at the home and office) at 65°F. or lower during winter months; and only heat the rooms you are using;

☐ using public transport. It's also much safer!

☐ using bicycles, carpools and, for trips under one mile, your feet;

☐ making dish washing a family time instead of buying a dishwasher.

4. Resist TV advertising by:

☐ turning down the sound, when commercials come on and

using the time to do something else, or talk about the programme you're watching. If it is not worth talking about is it worth watching?

5. Buy and renovate an old house in the inner city (and persuade a few friends to do the same so you can form a Christian community).

6. Reduce our society's consumption of nonrenewable natural resources by:

☐ resisting planned obsolescence (purchasing quality products when you must buy);

☐ sharing appliances, tools, lawnmowers, sports equipment, books, even a car (this is easier if you live close to other Christians committed to simple living);

☐ asking whether a car is really essential for you;

☐ organizing a "things closet" in your church for items used only occasionally—edger, clippers, camp beds for unexpected guests, lawnmowers, camping equipment, ladder.

7. Have one or two "home-made" babies and then adopt.

8. See how much of what you spend is for status and eliminate it.

9. Refuse to keep up with clothing fashions. (Virtually no reader of this book needs to buy any clothes—except maybe shoes—for two or three years.)

10. Find out what the supplementary benefit level is for you and your family and try living on it for three months.

11. Give your children and relations more of your love and time rather than more things.

12. Question all items of your expenditure.

Most Christians live at almost exactly the same standard of living as non-Christians with the same income. They share roughly the same expenditure pattern, except that the extra the non-Christian spends on alcohol, smoking, betting or various other activities, the Christian gives to the Lord's work. Their home/flat, its furnishings, the type of car they drive are all about the same as their non-Christian counterparts. Have you ever wondered why so many evangelical Christians are living in the rich outer suburbs of cities such as London, compared to how few are living in the poorer inner city areas? Is the Lord really calling us not only to live in the affluent quarter of the world, but also to live in the affluent half of that country as well? Perhaps the last part of a person to be converted is the pocket.

CRITERIA FOR GIVING If 10 per cent of all Western Christians adopted the graduated tithe, huge sums of money would become available for kingdom work. Where would that money do the most good?

Obviously Christians should not give all their money to relieve world hunger. Christian education and evangelism are extremely important and deserve continuing support. My family tries to give approximately as much to support evangelism as we do to activities promoting social justice. (What we like best are holistic programmes that combine both!) We regularly give some funds through nonchurch channels. Part of a graduated tithe might appropriately be given to political campaigns devoted to social justice.

But which relief and development agencies are doing the best job? That issue is extremely important, but you must decide for yourself. Here are some general criteria for deciding where to channel your giving for development in hungry lands:

1. Do the funds support holistic projects in the Third World working simultaneously at an integrated programme of evangelism, social change, education, agricultural development, and so on?

2. Do the funds support truly indigenous projects? That involves several issues: (a) Are the leaders and most of the staff of the projects in the developing nations indigenous persons? (They should be.) (b) Do the projects unthinkingly adopt Western ideas, materials and technology or do they carefully develop material suited to their own culture? (c) Did the project arise from the felt needs of the people rather than from some outside "expert"?

3. Are the projects primarily engaged in long-range development (that includes people development), or in brief emergency projects only?

4. Are the programmes designed to help the poor masses understand that God wants sinful social structures changed and that they can help effect that change?

5. Do the programmes grow out of and foster Christian community?

6. Are the programmes potentially self-supporting after an initial injection of seed capital? And do the programmes from the beginning require commitment and a significant contribution of capital or time (or both) from the people themselves?

7. Do the programmes aid the poorest people in the poorest developing countries?

8. Is agricultural development involved? (It need not always be, but in a majority of cases it should be.)

9. Is justice rather than continual charity the result?[13]

10. Several important questions can be asked of the agency through which one channels funds. How much is spent on administration and fund raising? Are the board and staff persons of known integrity? Is the board paid? (It should not be.) Are Third World and other minority persons and women represented among the board and top staff? Are staff salaries consistent with biblical teaching on economic relationships amongst the people of God? Did the organization object to answering these questions?

An example will help clarify the kind of holistic programme which meets most of the above criteria. This description comes from Jubilee Fund, a new evangelical organization supporting holistic development programmes in the Third World.

Elizabeth Native Interior Mission [is] in southern Liberia. ENI is headed by Augustus Marwieh who became a Christian under Mother George, one of the first black American missionaries to Africa. Ten years ago Gus went to work at the struggling mission where he had been saved. The young people were leaving the villages to go to the capital city of Monrovia; there, most found only un-employment, alcohol, and prostitution. Local skills like log sawing, blacksmithing, and making pottery were dying out as the people became dependent on outside traders (usually foreigners) and became poorer and poorer. At least 90 per cent of the people were illiterate, and many suffered from protein deficiency.

Today 160 churches have been started, and 10,000 people have become Christians. Eleven primary schools are operating, and they stress locally usable skills instead of the usual Liberian fare of Spot and Jane in English. A vocational school is forming that will help revive local trades and encourage new skills; and steps are being taken to form co-operatives which will avoid middlemen, replace foreign merchants, provide capital, etc.

One crucial element, especially in view of their protein shortage, is agriculture, and in the last ten years the people have made great strides. But they are so poor that often the only farming tool they have is a machete (a heavy knife). So Gus is burdened to start a revolving loan fund from which people can borrow to buy a hoe, a shovel, a water can, spraying equipment, a pick, or an axe. You and I buy tools like that on a whim for the garden in our back-yards, but for these people such purchases are completely out of reach even though they need them to fight malnutrition. So next time you start feeling poor, remember Gus' people, and send money to Jubilee Fund.[14]

There are scores of similar holistic programmes operated by biblical Christians in developing countries. And they desperately need additional funds. Organizations that enable us to share with them represent a contemporary way for God's people to live the Jubilee.

The gulf between what affluent Christians give and what they could give is a terrifying tragedy.

I have focussed on monetary giving in most of this chapter. But that is not the only way. Giving oneself is equally important. Some Christians choose low-paying jobs because the opportunity for service is great. Others decline overtime to permit more volunteer activity. Thousands of Christians have given two or more years to serve in developing countries.

There is a great need for sensitive persons who will live with the people in rural villages showing the poor that God wants them to help change the unjust structures which oppress them. Agricultural workers who can share intermediate technological skills are also in very high demand. "One person with practical skills who's prepared to work and live in a remote village is generally worth a dozen visiting university professors and business tycoons."[15] Time is money. Sharing time is just as important as sharing financial resources.

I am convinced that simpler living is a biblical imperative for contemporary Christians in affluent lands. But we must remain clear about our reasons. We are *not* committed to a simple lifestyle. We have only one absolute loyalty and that is to Jesus and his kingdom. But the head of this kingdom is the God of the poor! And hundreds of millions of his poor are starving.

An Age of Hunger summons affluent people to a lower standard of living. But a general assent to this statement will not be enough to escape the daily seductions of advertising. Each of us needs some *specific, concrete* plan. The graduated tithe and communal living offer two models. The example of Walt and Ginny Hearn suggests another. There are many more. By all means avoid legalism and self-righteousness. But have the courage to commit yourself to some *specific method* for moving toward a just personal lifestyle.

Will we dare to measure our living standards by the needs of the poor rather than by the lifestyle of our neighbours?

8 | WATCHING OVER ONE ANOTHER IN LOVE

EXTRA ECCLESIAM, NULLA SALUS. SOMEHOW THE PRESSURES OF MODERN SOCIETY WERE MAKING IT INCREASINGLY DIFFICULT FOR US TO LIVE BY THE VALUES WE HAD BEEN TAUGHT. WE THOUGHT OUR CHURCH SHOULD CONSTITUTE A COMMUNITY OF BELIEVERS CAPABLE OF WITHSTANDING THESE PRESSURES, YET IT SEEMED TO GO ALONG WITH THINGS AS THEY WERE INSTEAD OF ENCOURAGING AN ALTERNATIVE. THE "PILLARS" OF THE CHURCH SEEMED AS SEVERELY TRAPPED BY MATERIAL CONCERNS AND ALIENATION AS MOST NON-CHRISTIANS WE KNEW. [DAVE AND NETA JACKSON[1]]

The church should consist of communities of loving defiance. Instead it consists largely of comfortable clubs of conformity. A far-reaching reformation of the church is a prerequisite if it is to commit itself to Jesus' mission of liberating the oppressed.

If the analysis in the preceding chapters is even approximately correct, then the God of the Bible is calling Christians today to live in fundamental nonconformity to contemporary society. Affluent North American and European societies are obsessed with materialism, sex, economic success and military might. Things are more important than persons. Job security and an annual salary increase matter more than starving children and oppressed peasants. Paul's warning to the Romans is especially pertinent today: "Don't let the world around you squeeze you into its own mould" (Rom. 12:2, Philips). Biblical revelation summons us to defy many of the basic values of our materialistic, adulterous society.

But that is impossible! As individuals, that is. It is hardly possible for isolated believers to resist the anti-Christian values which pour forth from our radios, TV's and advertising hoardings. The values of our affluent society seep slowly and subtly into our hearts and minds. The only way to defy them is to immerse ourselves deeply in Christian fellowship so that God can fundamentally remould our thinking, as we find our primary identity with other brothers and sisters who are also unconditionally committed to biblical values.

That faithful obedience is possible only in the context of powerful Christian fellowship should not surprise us. The early church was able to defy the decadent values of Roman civilization precisely because it experienced the reality of Christian fellowship in a mighty way. For the early Christians *koinonia* was not the frilly "fellowship" of church-sponsored, biweekly outings. It was not tea, biscuits and sophisticated small-talk in Fellowship Hall after the sermon. It was an unconditional sharing of their lives with the other members of Christ's body.

Christian fellowship meant unconditional availability to and unlimited liability for the other sisters and brothers—emotionally, financially and spiritually. When one member suffered, they all suffered. When one rejoiced, they all rejoiced (1 Cor. 12:26). When a person or church experienced economic trouble, the others shared without reservation.[2] And when a brother or sister fell into sin, the others gently restored the straying person (Mt. 18:15–17; 1 Cor. 5; 2 Cor. 2:5–11; Gal. 6:1–3).[3] The sisters and brothers were available to each other, liable for each other and accountable to each other.

The early church, of course, did not always fully live out the New Testament vision of the body of Christ. There were tragic lapses. But the network of tiny house churches scattered throughout the Roman Empire did experience their oneness in

Christ so vividly that they were able to defy and eventually conquer a powerful, pagan civilization.

John Wesley's early Methodist class meetings captured something of the spirit alive in the early church. These assembled in houses weekly, bringing together persons "united in order to pray together, to receive the word of exhortation, and to watch over one another in love, that they may help each other to work out their salvation".[4] The overwhelming majority of churches today, however, do not provide the context in which brothers and sisters can encourage, admonish and disciple each other. We desperately need new settings and structures for watching over one another in love.

A SOCIOLOGICAL PERSPECTIVE The sociology of knowledge underlines the importance of Christian community for biblical nonconformists. Sociologists of knowledge have studied the relationship between ideas and the social conditions in which ideas arise. They have discovered that the plausibility of ideas depends on the social support they have. "We obtain our notions about the world originally from other human beings, and these notions continue to be plausible to us in a very large measure because others continue to affirm them."[5] An Amish youth who migrates to New York City will soon begin to question earlier values. The sociological reason for this change is that the "significant others" who previously supported his ideas and values are no longer present.

The complicated network of social interactions in which one develops and maintains one's view of reality is called a plausibility structure. This plausibility structure consists of ongoing conversation with "significant others" as well as specific practices, rituals and legitimations designed to support the validity of certain ideas. As long as these social processes continue, we tend to accept the corresponding beliefs as true or plausible. But if the supportive structures disappear, doubt and uncertainty arise.

Hence the difficulty of a cognitive minority. A cognitive minority is a small group of people who hold a set of beliefs that differ sharply from the majority in their society. Because they constantly meet people who challenge their fundamental ideas, members of a cognitive minority find it very difficult to maintain their distinctive beliefs. According to well-known sociologist Peter Berger, a cognitive minority can maintain its unpopular ideas only if it has a strong community structure:

Unless our theologian has the inner fortitude of a desert saint, he has only one effective remedy against the threat of cognitive collapse in the face of these pressures. He must huddle together with like-minded fellow deviants—and huddle very closely indeed. Only in a counter-community of considerable strength does cognitive deviance have a chance to maintain itself. The counter-community provides continuing therapy against the creeping doubt as to whether, after all, one may not be wrong and the majority right. To fulfil its function of providing social support for the deviant body of "knowledge," the countercommunity must provide a strong sense of solidarity among its members.[6]

Berger's analysis relates directly to contemporary Christians determined to follow biblical teaching on the poor and possessions. Berger analysed the problem of orthodox Christians who defy the dominant "scientific" ideas of contemporary secularism and maintain a biblical belief in the supernatural. But his analysis pertains just as clearly to the problem of living the ethics of Jesus' kingdom in a world that follows different standards. Most of our contemporaries—both inside and outside the churches—accept the dominant values of our consumption-oriented, materialistic culture. Genuine Christians, on the other hand, are committed to the very different norms revealed in Scripture. It should not surprise us that only a faithful remnant continues to cling to these values. But the fact that genuine Christians are a cognitive minority alerts us to the need for strong Christian community.

That does not mean that Christians should imitate the Amish and retreat to isolated rural solitude. We must remain at the very centre of contemporary society in order to challenge, witness against and, hopefully, change it. But precisely as we are in the world, but not of it, the pressure to abandon biblical norms in favour of contemporary values will be intense. Hence the need for new forms of Christian community today.

The ancient Catholic dictum, *extra ecclesiam nulla salus* ("outside the church there is no salvation") contains a significant sociological truth. Certainly it is not impossible for individual Christians to maintain biblical beliefs even if a hostile majority disagrees. But if the church is to consist of communities of loving defiance in a sinful world, then it must pay more attention to the quality of its fellowship.

What are some promising models of Christian community for our time?

NEW PATTERNS OF CHRISTIAN COMMUNITY

When one speaks of Christian "community," some people instantly think of Christian communes. That is unfortunate. Communes are only one of many faithful forms for genuine Christian fellowship today. House churches or mission groups within larger congregations, individual house churches and very small traditional churches all offer excellent contexts for living out the biblical vision of the church.

I am thoroughly convinced, however, that the overwhelming majority of Western churches no longer understand or experience biblical *koinonia* to any significant degree. As mentioned earlier, the essence of Christian community is unconditional accountability to and unlimited liability for our sisters and brothers in the body of Christ. That means that our time, our money and our very selves are available to the brothers and sisters.

That kind of fellowship hardly ever happens in larger churches of one hundred or more persons. It requires small communities of believers like the early Christian house churches. The movement which conquered the Roman Empire was a network of small house churches. Frequently Paul speaks of "the church that meets in the house of . . ." (Rom. 16:5, 23; 1 Cor. 16:19; Col. 4:15; Phil. 2; see also Acts 2:46; 12:12; 20:7–12). It was only in the latter part of the third century that the church started to build sanctuaries. The structure of the early church fostered close interaction and fellowship.[7]

What happens when God grants the gift of genuine Christian fellowship? Deep joyful sharing replaces the polite prattle typically exchanged by Christians on Sunday morning. Sisters and brothers begin to discuss the things that really matter to them. They disclose their inner fears, their areas of peculiar temptation and their deepest joys. And they begin to challenge and disciple each other according to Matthew 18:15–17 and Galatians 6:1–3.

It is in that kind of setting—and perhaps only in that kind of setting—that the church today will be able to forge a faithful lifestyle for Christians in an Age of Hunger. In small house church settings brothers and sisters can challenge each others' affluent lifestyles. They can discuss family finances and evaluate each others' annual budgets. Larger expenditures (like houses, cars and long holidays) can be evaluated honestly in terms of the needs of both the individuals involved and God's poor around the world. Tips for simple living can be shared. Voting patterns that liberate the poor, jobs that are ecologically responsible and charitable donations that build self-reliance among the oppressed—these and many other issues can be discussed openly and honestly by persons who have pledged themselves to each other as brothers and sisters in Christ.

What models of the church foster that kind of Christian community?

A CONGREGATION OF HOUSE CHURCHES Congregations composed of clusters of house churches make up an exciting, viable alternative to the typical congregation today. Living Word Community in Philadelphia and the Church of the Saviour in Washington are two variations on this theme.

Eight years ago Living Word Community (formerly Gospel Temple) was a typical, successful Pentecostal church. There was a large, growing congregation of several hundred people from the greater Philadelphia area. The church had a young dynamic pastor, a packed schedule of meetings, a full repertoire of church organizations and, according to the pastor, little real Christian fellowship.

In 1970 it decided to change drastically. The church jettisoned all existing activities except the Sunday morning worship service. Everyone was urged to attend "Home Meetings" where twelve to twenty people met weekly for study, prayer, worship and shepherding. For a couple of years, the pastor reported, they often feared that they had made a gigantic mistake. "To move from a pew to a living room chair and look at people face to face was terrifying."[8] But a breakthrough occurred when the leaders of the home meetings realized that most people did not know how to meet each other's needs. The leaders started making suggestions: "You two ladies go to Jane Brown's house and make dinner for her because she is sick." "You three people paint Jerry's apartment on Saturday."

Oneness and caring began to develop. These weekly gatherings became the centre of spiritual activity in the church. Counselling, discipling, even evangelistic outreach all began to happen primarily in the home meetings. One result was rapid growth. As soon as a home meeting reached twenty-five persons it was divided into two home meetings.

In 1974 growth had already led to division into two weekend services. By 1976 thirteen to fourteen hundred people were attending weekend services. There were fifty different home meetings and four separate "Sunday" services.

One of these four weekend gatherings still occurs on Sunday morning in the original downtown sanctuary. For the others, the congregation rents space from various churches and holds the weekend service on Saturday or Sunday evening. As a result the congregation has avoided costly building programmes and has financial resources available for more important matters.

Genuine Christian community has emerged from this drastic restructuring. Because of the small home meetings, the leaders confidently assert that all eight hundred members of Living Word Community receive personal, pastoral care. Each individual's burdens and problems are known in his or her small home meeting.

Financial sharing was not part of the original vision. But it has begun to happen in a significant way. Members of home meetings recently dug into savings and stocks to provide interest-free loans for two families who purchased house trailers for homes. When members went to sign the papers for an interest-free mortgage for another family's house, the others present for the transfer were totally perplexed! If a member of a home meeting needs small amounts of financial assistance ($50 or $100), the other members of his home meeting help out. A congregational fund meets larger needs. Plans for food co-ops and a store for used clothing and furniture are being developed. A sizable portion (30 per cent in a recent year) of total congregational giving is used for economic sharing in the church.

Living Word Community has not yet developed an extensive concern for justice and the poor. But it has begun. The pastor preaches about social justice. The church has shared substantially with an inner-city black congregation. 10 per cent of gross church revenues go to relieve world poverty. A deeper commitment to simpler lifestyles and more understanding of injustice in economic structures is needed. But it is probable that these concerns can develop at Living Word Community. The creative upheaval of the last six years has produced a flexible openness to new directions in discipleship. And the small house-church structure is an ideal context in which to forge new economic lifestyles.

Living Word Community has demonstrated that a traditional congregation can be transformed into a cluster of house churches. And the result has been not destructive disruption but growth—in discipleship, Christian community and numbers.

Washington, D.C.'s Church of the Saviour pioneered the small group model at the end of World War Two.[9] All members must be in one of the twenty mission groups. Prospective members must take five classes over a period of about two years. The membership covenant, renewed annually, commits every member to four disciplines: daily prayer, daily Bible study, weekly worship and proportionate giving, beginning with a tithe of total gross income.

Consisting of five to twelve persons, the mission groups are the heart of the Church of the Saviour. They are not merely prayer cells, Bible study gatherings, encounter groups or social action committees (although they are all of these). Gordon Cosby, pastor of Church of the Saviour, underlines the fact that it is in the mission groups that the members experience the reality of the body of Christ: "The mission group embodies the varied dimensions of church. It is total in scope. It is both inward and outward. It requires that we be accountable to Christ and to one another for the totality of our lives. It assumes

that we share unlimited liability for one another."[10] Via verbal
or written reports, each member of a mission group reports
weekly on failure or success in following the covenanted
disciplines, on new scriptural insight, and on problems and
joys of the week.

Economics figures prominently in the membership commitment. Part of the membership covenant reads:

*I believe that God is the total owner of my life and resources. I
give God the throne in relation to the material aspect of my life.
God is the owner. I am the ower. Because God is a lavish giver, I
too shall be lavish and cheerful in my regular gifts.*[11]

The church has held out the goal of accountability of brothers
and sisters to each other in the use of personal finances. Some
mission groups regularly share income tax returns as a basis
for discussing each other's family budgets and finances. Concern for more simple lifestyles is growing at Church of the
Saviour.

The goal of many of the mission groups is liberation for the
poor. Members of the mission group called Jubilee Housing
renovate deteriorating housing in inner-city Washington.
Along with another mission group (Jubilee Neighbours), they
are bringing hope of genuine change to one block of five
hundred persons. The Polycultural Institute Mission will
bring together students from many nations to study world
problems such as hunger, racism and nationalism. For Love
of Children has fought for the rights of neglected children
through court action, legislation, and monitoring local and
federal governmental activity.

Dunamis is one of the best known mission groups. Different
task forces in this group select specific public policy issues (one
is world hunger) and build relationships of love, prayer and
prophetic witness with members of Congress. Recently the
Dunamis concept of pastoral-prophetic relationships with
public figures has been expanded to state and local government
in other parts of the country.[12]

By 1976 increasing size seemed to threaten genuine community at the church. (There were one hundred members
plus fifty intern members!) As a result the church is dividing
into four, fully autonomous sister communities. If, as Gordon

Cosby hopes, these new communities have a wide economic mix, the growing concern for economic sharing and simple living will undoubtedly increase. Like Living Word Community in Philadelphia, the Church of the Saviour prefers to subdivide into small congregations rather than run the risk of diluting Christian community.

Though the numerous small groups flourishing in the churches today are useful and valuable, they seldom go far enough. Participants may agree to share deeply in one or two areas of life, but they do not assume responsibility for the other brothers' and sisters' growth toward Christian maturity in every area of life. Hardly ever do they dream that truly being sisters and brothers in Christ means unlimited economic liability for each other or responsibility for the economic lifestyles of the other members! The crucial question is: Have the participants committed themselves to be brothers and sisters to each other so unreservedly that they are unconditionally liable for and accountable to each other? Almost everyone expects most small groups to dissolve in six months or two years. Life will then continue as before. They are "limited liability" small groups. They have genuine importance. But what people desperately need today is the church. From the biblical perspective, being the church means accepting unconditional liability for and total availability and accountability to the other members of the local expression of Christ's body.

There are a few churches in Britain which have gone some way towards this, with the concept of "extended families". One of the best-known is St. Cuthbert's, York. There, several "nuclear" family units are enlarged to provide homes for a few single people, for whom loneliness might otherwise be a major problem.

The same idea was one of the reasons for the formation of the Community of the Word of God in Hackney, East London, in 1972. Prebendary John Pearce, an Anglican clergyman, and his wife saw many Christian people, mainly single women, finding themselves unable to cope as Christians in the East End without close supporting fellowship, and consequently having to leave the area. Wondering how to prevent this exit of the Christian presence in Hackney, the Pearces' original concept was a community of women. Later, it became clear that men wished to join and, later still, married couples.

The other basic strand in their thinking was the community concept of the early church (as related in Acts 2.44: "All who believed were together and had all things in common"). Commitment to God and to each other means, for them, the sharing of all monetary income, homes, food and friendship. Not a church in itself, this community is linked very closely with the local Anglican church.

THE INDIVIDUAL HOUSE CHURCH Another structure where true Christian community can happen is the individual house church. Virtually no expenses are involved. When it is impossible to find genuine Christian community in any other way, small groups of Christians should begin meeting in their own homes. (But they should promptly seek a relationship with other bodies of Christians. Lone rangers are not God's will for his church!) In his recent book on church structures, Howard A. Snyder proposes that denominations adopt the house church model for church planting, especially in the city. This structure is flexible, mobile, inclusive and personal. It can grow by division, is an effective means of evangelism and needs little professional leadership.[13]

An ideal house church arrangement is to have several families and/or single persons purchase houses near each other. Living across the street or down the road from each other can greatly facilitate sharing such things as cars, washing machines or gardening equipment. Living close together also encourages Christian community.

THE CHRISTIAN COMMUNE Thousands of communal experiments have occurred in the last decade. Many have been explicitly Christian. The Christian commune represents an alternative model for persons dissatisfied with our consumer-oriented society.

Reba Place Fellowship in Evanston, Illinois, began with three people in 1957.[14] Today over one hundred and fifty persons live in about a dozen households of ten to twenty persons each.

Reba Place practices total economic sharing. Members place

their earnings in a common treasury. The central fund pays directly for large expenditures like housing, utilities and transportation. Each month, every family and single person receives an allowance for food, clothing and incidentals. The food allowance is the same as that for persons on welfare in Chicago. Because of the size and permanence of the community, no insurance is necessary (except that required by law). Not channelling cash into the rich insurance industry frees considerable money for other things. Household living also requires "fewer automobiles, washing machines, lawnmowers, BTUs of heat, electric lights, square feet of floor space, TVs, stereos, stoves and refrigerators."[15] The simple lifestyle at Reba Place enables this community to share generously with the poor in the immediate community and around the world.

But Reba Place is not just an economic commune. It is a local body of Christian believers. A recent incident suggests the character of their total availability to each other.

One day a man with a serious drinking problem dropped in to talk with Virgil Vogt, one of the elders. When Virgil invited him to accept Christ and join the community of believers, the man grew uncomfortable and hastily insisted that he simply wanted money for a bus ticket to Cleveland!

"O.K." Virgil agreed, "we can give that kind of help too, if that's all you really want." He was quiet a moment, then he shook his head. "You know something?" he said, looking straight at the man. "You've just really let me off the hook. Because if you had chosen a new way of life in the kingdom of God, then as your brother I would have had to lay down my whole life for you. This house, my time, all my money, whatever you needed to meet your needs would have been totally at your disposal for the rest of your life. But all you want is some money for a bus ticket . . ." The man was so startled he stood up and shortly left, without remembering to take the money. The next Sunday he was sitting next to Virgil in the worship service.[16]

Reba Place and other Christian communities, like the Episcopal Church of the Redeemer in Houston (see Chapter 7), offer a setting in which unconditional liability for and accountability to other brothers and sisters can become a reality.[17]

The Bible and the daily newspaper issue the same summons.

Faithful people in an Age of Hunger must adopt simple life-styles and change unjust economic structures. But that is not a popular path to tread in an affluent society. Unless Christians anchor themselves in genuine Christian community, they will be unable to live the radical nonconformity commanded by Scripture and essential in our time. Our only hope is a return to the New Testament's vision of the body of Christ. If that happens the Lord of the church may again create communities of loving defiance able to withstand and conquer powerful, pagan civilizations of East and West worshipping at the shrine of Mammon.

Appropriation of the biblical teaching on the church as a new community can also help us avoid one of the most glaring weaknesses of much Christian social action of the past few decades. To ask the government to legislate what the church cannot persuade its members to live is a tragic absurdity. Unfortunately, church leaders have often done precisely that.

A meeting of church leaders held in the Chicago area in the 1960's illustrates the problem. Blacks were marching to demand an end to de facto housing segregation. Wanting to help, the clergy met to devise a strategy for bringing pressure on the city's business and political leadership to yield to black demands. After listening for an hour or so to various economic and political schemes, someone raised a question. Were not the bank presidents and the mayor active church members? They were, the clergy agreed—but they were puzzled at this irrelevant query. It was not at all obvious to those concerned clergy that the church must demonstrate in its common life together what it calls on secular society to embody in public policy.

Today's movement of concern among church people for world hunger and injustice in the international economic order is in danger of repeating the same mistake. Economic relationships in our Lord's worldwide body today constitute a desecration of his body and blood. Only as groups of believers in North America and Europe dare to incarnate in their life together what the Bible teaches about economic relationships among the people of God do they have any right to demand that leaders in Washington or Westminster shape a new world economic order.

We must confess the tragic sinfulness of present economic relationships in the worldwide body of Christ. While our brothers and sisters in the Third World ache for lack of minimal health care, minimal education, even just enough food to escape starvation, Christians in the northern hemisphere grow richer each year—like the Corinthian Christians who feasted without sharing their food with the poor members of the church (1 Cor. 11:20–29). Like them we fail today to discern the reality of Christ's body.

As we shall see in the next chapter, this emphasis on simpler personal and ecclesiastical lifestyles is by no means intended to belittle the importance of changing public policy. (Note, however, that living the new model would deeply affect the economy; and the powerful example of sharing could also profoundly influence the thinking and lifestyle of non-Christians.) Certainly we should strengthen organizations working to change public policy. Certainly we should work politically to demand costly concessions from Washington and Westminster in international forums working to reshape the International Monetary Fund and forge new policy in trade negotiations on tariffs, commodity agreements and the like. However, our attempt to restructure secular society will possess integrity only if our personal lifestyles—and our corporate ecclesiastical practices in local congregations, in regions and denominations, and in the worldwide body of Christians—demonstrate that we are already daring to live what we ask governments to legislate.

A radical call to repentance so that the church becomes the church must be central to Christian strategies for reducing world hunger and restructuring international economic relationships. The church is the most universal body in the world today. It has the opportunity to live a new corporate model of economic sharing at a desperate moment in world history. If even one-tenth of the Christians in the northern hemisphere had the courage to live the biblical vision of economic equality among the people of God, the governments of our dangerously divided global village might also be persuaded to legislate the sweeping changes needed to avert disaster.

STRUCTURAL CHANGE

THE PRESENT SOCIAL ORDER IS THE MOST ABJECT FAILURE THE WORLD HAS EVER SEEN ... GOVERNMENTS HAVE NEVER LEARNED YET HOW TO SO LEGISLATE AS TO DISTRIBUTE THE FRUITS OF THE INDUSTRY OF THEIR PEOPLE. THE COUNTRIES OF THE EARTH PRODUCE ENOUGH TO SUPPORT ALL, AND IF THE EARNINGS OF EACH WAS FAIRLY DISTRIBUTED IT WOULD MAKE ALL MEN TOIL SOME, BUT NO MAN TOIL TOO MUCH. THIS GREAT CIVILIZATION OF OURS HAS NOT LEARNED SO TO DISTRIBUTE THE PRODUCT OF HUMAN TOIL SO THAT IT SHALL BE EQUITABLY HELD. THEREFORE, THE GOVERNMENT BREAKS DOWN, [C. I. SCOFIELD, AUTHOR OF THE SCOFIELD BIBLE NOTES, 1903.[1]]

A group of devout Christians once lived in a small village at the foot of a mountain. A winding, slippery road with hairpin curves and steep precipices without guard rails wound its way up one side of the mountain and down the other. There were frequent fatal accidents. Deeply saddened by the injured people who were pulled from the wrecked cars, the Christians in the village's three churches decided to act. They pooled their resources and purchased an ambulance so that they could rush the injured to the hospital in the next town. Week after week church volunteers gave faithfully, even sacrificially, of their time to operate the ambulance twenty-four hours a day. They saved many lives although some victims remained crippled for life.

Then one day a visitor came to town. Puzzled, he asked why they did not close the road over the mountain and build a tunnel instead. Startled at first, the ambulance volunteers quickly pointed out that this approach (although technically quite possible) was not realistic or advisable. After all, the narrow mountain road had been there for a long time. Besides, the mayor would bitterly oppose the idea. (He owned a large restaurant and service station halfway up the mountain.)

The visitor was shocked that the mayor's economic interests mattered more to these Christians than the many human casualties. Somewhat hesitantly, he suggested that perhaps the churches ought to speak to the mayor. After all, he was an elder in the oldest church in town. Perhaps they should even elect a different mayor if he proved stubborn and unconcerned. Now the Christians were shocked. With rising indignation and righteous conviction they informed the young radical that the church dare not become involved in politics. The church is called to preach the gospel and give a cup of cold water. Its mission is not to dabble in worldly things like changing social and political structures.

Perplexed and bitter, the visitor left. As he wandered out of the village, one question churned round and round in his muddled mind. Is it really more spiritual, he wondered, to operate the ambulances which pick up the bloody victims of destructive social structures than to try to change the structures themselves?

An Age of Hunger demands compassionate action and simplicity in personal lifestyles. But compassion and simple living apart from structural change may be little more than a gloriously irrelevant ego-trip or proud pursuit of personal purity.

Eating less beef or even becoming a vegetarian will not necessarily feed one starving child. If millions of Americans and Europeans reduce their beef consumption, but do not act politically to change public policy, the result will not necessarily be less starvation in the Third World. To be sure, if people give the money saved to private agencies promoting rural development in poor nations, then the result will be less hunger. But unless one also changes public policy, the primary effect of merely reducing one's meat consumption may simply be to enable the Russians to buy more grain at a cheaper price next year or to persuade farmers to plant less wheat. What is needed is a change in public policy. Our Age of Hunger demands structural change.

Many questions promptly arise. Granted, some structural change is necessary, but is our present economic system basically just or do Christians need to work for fundamental restructuring? And what specific structural changes consistent with biblical principles should Christians promote today? Are these principles even pertinent to *secular* society? Israel, after all, was a theocracy. And can we really expect unbelievers to live according to biblical ethics?

The Bible does not directly answer these questions. We do not find a comprehensive blueprint for a new economic order in Scripture, although biblical revelation tells us that God and his faithful people are always at work liberating the oppressed, and also provides some principles apropos of justice in society.

Certainly the first application of biblical truth concerning just relationships among God's people should be to the church. As the new people of God,[2] the church should be a new society incarnating the biblical principles on justice in society through its common life. Indeed only as the church itself is a visible model of transformed socio-economic relationships will any appeal to government possess integrity. Much recent Christian social action has been ineffective because Christian leaders called on the government to legislate what they could not persuade their church members to practice voluntarily.

Biblical principles also apply to secular societies, however, in a second, very important way. God did not arbitrarily dictate social norms for his people. The Creator revealed certain principles and social patterns because he knew what would lead to lasting peace and happiness for his creatures. Following biblical principles on justice in society is the only way to lasting peace and social harmony for all human societies.

The biblical vision of the coming kingdom suggests the kind

of social order God wills. And the church is supposed to be a living model now (imperfect, to be sure) of what the final kingdom of perfect justice and peace will be like. That means that the closer any secular society comes to the biblical norms for just relationships among the people of God, the more peace, happiness and harmony that society will enjoy. Obviously, sinful persons and societies will never get beyond a dreadfully imperfect approximation. But social structures do exert a powerful influence on saint and sinner alike. Christians, therefore, should exercise political influence to implement change in society at large.

The fact that the biblical authors did not hesitate to apply revealed norms to persons and societies outside the people of God supports this point. Amos announced divine punishment of the surrounding nations for their evil and injustice (Amos 1—2). Isaiah denounced Assyria for its pride and injustice (Is. 10:12–19). The Book of Daniel shows that God removed pagan kings like Nebuchadnezzar in the same way that he destroyed Israel's rulers when they failed to show mercy to the oppressed (Dan. 4:27). God obliterated Sodom and Gomorrah no less than Israel and Judah because they neglected to aid the poor and feed the hungry (Ezek. 16:49). As the Lord of the universe, Yahweh applies the same standards of social justice to all nations.

WHO WILL BE HELPED? But now we must face a very complex question: Given the present situation in developing countries, who would benefit from changes such as a new Western food policy or more just patterns of international trade? Would the poorest half of the developing countries be significantly better off? Not necessarily. North Americans and Europeans are not to blame for all the poverty in the world today. Many developing countries are ruled by tiny, wealthy elites largely unconcerned with the suffering of the masses in their lands. They often own a large percentage of the best land. They produce export crops to earn foreign exchange so they can buy luxury goods from the developed world. Meanwhile, the poorest 30 to 70 per cent of the people face grinding poverty.

It is a tragic fact that more foreign aid and improved trading patterns for developing countries would not necessarily improve the lot of the poorest in a significant way. Such changes might simply enable the wealthy elites to purchase more luxury goods and strengthen their repressive regimes.

But that does not mean that North Americans and Europeans can wash their hands of the whole problem. In many cases the wealthy elites continue in power because they receive massive military aid and diplomatic support from the United States and other industrial nations.[3] The United States has trained large numbers of police who have tortured thousands of people working for social justice in countries like Chile and Brazil.[4] Western-based multinational corporations work very closely with the repressive governments. Events in Brazil and Chile demonstrate that the United States will support dictatorships that use torture and do little for the poorest one-half as long as these regimes are friendly to U.S. investments.

What can be done? Western citizens must demand a drastic reorientation of Western foreign policy. We must demand a foreign policy that unequivocally sides with the poor. If we truly believe that all people are created equal, then our foreign policy must be redesigned to promote the interests of all people and not just the wealthy elites in developing countries or our own multinational corporations. We should use our economic and diplomatic power to push for change in Third World dictatorships, especially those like Argentina, Brazil, Chile, Iran, the Philippines, and Uruguay that make use of torture. (In the first two years of his administration President Carter has championed the cause of human rights in a new way.)[5]

We should also insist that foreign aid go only to countries seriously committed to improving the lot of the poorest portions of the population. Britain took an important step in this direction with the publication of a White Paper in Autumn 1975, under the direction of Judith Hart, the Minister for Overseas Development, called "More Help for the Poorest". This document seeks to concentrate aid on the poorest people in developing countries, particularly those in rural areas.[6] The World Bank says that it is also trying to concentrate its aid on the poorest developing countries and on the poorest people within developing countries. But careful analysis of its financial report for the year ending June 30, 1977 reveals only modest success thus far.[7]

We should openly encourage nonviolent movements working for structural change in developing countries. Western foreign policy ought to encourage justice rather than injustice. Only then will proposed changes in international trade, food policy and foreign aid actually improve the lot of the poorest billion.

A fundamental change in Western policy toward the developing nations is imperative, but it is not enough. In addition, the poor masses in developing nations must be encouraged to demand sweeping structural changes in their own lands. In a recent scholarly book on land tenure in India, Professor Robert Frykenberg of the University of Wisconsin lamented the growing gulf between rich and poor. "No amount of aid, science, and/or technology," he concluded, "can alter the direction of current processes without the occurrence of a more fundamental 'awakening' or 'conversion' among significantly larger numbers of people... Changes of a revolutionary character are required, changes which can only begin in the hearts and minds of individuals."[8]

It is precisely at this point that the Christian church—and missionaries in particular—can play a crucial role. To be sure, missionaries cannot engage directly in political activity in foreign countries. But they can and must teach the whole Word for the whole person. Why have missionaries so often taught Romans but not Amos to new converts in poor lands? If it is true, as we discovered in part two, that Scripture constantly asserts that God is on the side of the poor, then missionaries should make this biblical theme a central part of their teaching. If we accept our Lord's Great Commission to teach "all that I have commanded you", then we dare not omit or de-emphasize the biblical message of justice for the oppressed, even if it offends ruling elites in the countries concerned.

Cross-cultural missionaries need not engage directly in politics. But they must carefully and fully expound for new converts the explosive biblical message that God is on the side of the poor and oppressed. The poor will learn quickly how to apply biblical principles to their own oppressive societies. The result will be changed social structures in developing countries.

What are the fundamental biblical principles we need to keep in mind as we think of structural change in society? The most basic theological presupposition, of course, is that the sovereign Lord of this universe is always at work liberating the poor and oppressed and destroying the rich and mighty because of their injustice (Lk. 1:52, 53). God is on the side of the poor (see chapter 3). As the people of God become co-workers in this task of liberation, revealed principles on justice in society will shape their thought and action.

In Part Two I examined the biblical perspective on the poor and possessions. A brief reminder of some of the basic principles we discovered will help us in this chapter. Extremes of wealth and poverty are displeasing to the God of the Bible. Yahweh wills institutionalized structures (rather than mere charity) which systematically and regularly reduce the gap between the rich and the poor. Although they do not suggest a wooden, legalistic egalitarianism, the biblical patterns for economic sharing (for example, the Jubilee and the Pauline collection) all push toward a closer approximation of economic equality. People are vastly more valuable than property. Private property is legitimate. But since God is the only absolute owner, our right to acquire and use property is definitely limited. The human right to the resources necessary to earn a just living overrides any notion of absolute private ownership.

This last principle bears directly on the issues of this chapter. Some countries like the United States, Russia and Australia have a bountiful supply of natural resources within their national boundaries. Do they have an absolute right to use these resources as they please solely for the advantage of their own citizens? Not according to the Bible! If we believe Scripture, then we must conclude that the human right of all persons to earn a just living clearly supersedes the right of the developed nations to use our natural resources for ourselves. We are only stewards, not absolute owners. God is the absolute owner, and he insists that the earth's resources be shared.

Before sketching specific steps for applying these principles, I must register a disclaimer. We must constantly remember the large gulf between revealed principles and contemporary application. There are many valid ways to apply biblical principles. The application of biblical norms to socio-economic questions today leaves room for creativity and honest disagreement among biblical Christians. Objecting to my application of biblical ethics to contemporary society is not at all the same as rejecting biblical principles. That does not mean that all applications are equally valid; it does mean that humility and tolerance are imperative. We can and must help each other see where we are unfaithful to biblical revelation and biased by our economic self-interest. Scripture, as always, is the norm.

What then are some practical steps in addition to the crucial change in foreign policy already discussed?

INTERNATIONAL TRADE We saw in Chapter 6 that industrialized nations have carefully manipulated international trade to their economic advantage. They have erected tariff barriers and other trade restrictions to keep out manufactured products exported by developing countries. And they have been very slow to correct the violent fluctuations of prices of primary products exported by developing nations, and these prices have declined sharply in real terms over the last twenty-five years. International trade accounts for at least 80 per cent of all the money that flows from rich to poor nations. Hence higher prices for their products would benefit the poor countries immensely. Brazilian Archbishop Dom Helder Camara speaks for all developing nations: "It is not aid that we need . . . If the affluent countries, East and West, Europe and the United States, are willing to pay fair prices to the developing countries for their natural resources, they can keep their aid and their relief plans."[9]

Developed nations should drastically reduce or eliminate trade barriers on imports from developing nations. The long-standing Western policy of increasing import duties in proportion to the amount of processing and manufacturing the product has undergone, has hindered industrial growth in the Third World. The rate of effective protection afforded by such a policy is of course much higher than the nominal rate of tariff.[10]

On January 1, 1976 the United States took a significant step forward. It granted tariff preferences for manufactured products from developing nations. As the *Wall Street Journal* pointed out, however, the change affected a mere one-fifth of all goods imported by the United States from developing nations.[11] In its annual survey, the Overseas Development Council concluded that the new tariff preferences were quite inadequate:

The generalized tariff preferences extended to them [the developing countries] by the United States and other developed countries . . . continue to be severely limited both in terms of product coverage and product-by-product volume coverage. Mainly because of pressures for protection within all of the larger industrial societies, many of the products that the developing countries are most able to export are not eligible for preferences; in the cases of many of their other products, volume limitations established by legislative or administrative actions appear to offer little incentive to develop an export capacity that would achieve optimal scales of production.[12]

A far more sweeping elimination of tariff barriers is needed.

But such a change will not happen unless citizens concerned about hungry people demand it. In his book, *Economic Development*, Professor Theodore Morgan emphasizes the fact that the removal of tariff barriers would be "very helpful" to developing nations. But he concludes on a pessimistic note: "Experience to date suggests that domestic pressure in MDCs [more developed countries] from firms and worker organizations will make concessions as modest in the future as they have been in the past."[13] Those who believe that God is on the side of the poor must defy such pessimism and vested interests, and try to effect the necessary political changes!

As developed nations eliminate trade barriers to products from the developing countries, two things will be necessary. Developed nations will need to grant trade preferences to developing nations and also permit them to protect their infant industries with tariffs for a time. Developed nations will also need to have some mechanism so that people thrown out of work by cheaper foreign imports do not bear this burden alone. All citizens must share the costs of job retraining and industrial readjustment.

Two of the most important demands of developing countries in their proposals for a New International Economic Order were: (1) a Common Fund for commodities to help stabilize prices (by avoiding wild price fluctuations) and to see that the prices of primary products rose in line with the prices of manufactured goods which developing nations must purchase from developed nations (indexing was a proposed mechanism); (2) generalised debt relief. At the fourth meeting of the United Nations Conference on Trade and Development (UNCTAD IV) at Nairobi in May 1976, the developed and developing world failed to agree on debt relief and a Common Fund for commodities, largely because of opposition from the U.S., Germany and Japan. They argued that a Common Fund for commodities would disturb the "free market" in these commodities.

Talks on these issues were continued at the Conference on International Economic Cooperation (C.I.E.C.) commonly known as the North-South dialogue at the end of May 1977, between nineteen developing countries (seven oil exporting states and twelve others) and eight industrialized states (the E.E.C. counting as one). Originally the industrialized nations intended the talks to be only about energy. But the developing countries, with the help of the oil exporters, successfully extended the talks to cover wider issues such as commodities and debt relief. The issue of the Common Fund was singled out by the developing countries as a key test case of the industrialized countries' willingness to change the international economic order in their favour. Western objections to the Fund shifted from outright rejection by the U.S. and West Germany (the U.S. position had changed earlier in the year as a result of the new Carter administration but the West Germans didn't finally lift their objections till the conference itself) as running counter to market forces, to fears that it would push up commodity prices to unrealistic levels. The West argued that buffer stocks are suited only to certain commodities like tin, rubber, coffee and cocoa, and that the $6 billion sought by the developing nations for the Fund was dangerously excessive.

During the Paris conference the developing countries also asked for a cancellation of debts for the least developed, some relief for those considered "most seriously affected" and a conference of debtors and creditors which would include on its agenda the renegotiation of commercial debts. The Third World demand for a complete moratorium on their international debt payments was however turned down by the West. But the rich countries did offer an extra $1,000 million to help the very poorest nations, and promised to look at debt relief on a case by case basis.

Although there is some debate among economists, the above suggestions seem just and desirable. Though very modest in comparison to the year of Jubilee, they, like it, would be institutionalized mechanisms for reducing extremes of wealth and poverty. More extensive means for implementing the Jubilee principle are also needed. But even the ones discussed will become a reality only if citizens in affluent nations demand that their governments pay the price.

More just international trade patterns will cost affluent consumers a good deal. Consequently they will not be implemented unless citizens inform their elected officials that they are willing to pay the cost of international justice.

A NEW FOOD POLICY North America, Lester Brown informs us, has virtually "monopolistic control of the world's exportable grain supplies".[14] The percentage of all international grain exports controlled by the United States, Canada and Australia is much higher than the percentage of oil exports controlled by the OPEC countries. The record harvests of 1975–77 have eased the world food situation from the desperate shortages that characterized 1972–1974 and led to a tripling of grain prices. But many experts predict that worldwide grain shortages will reappear and by 1985, the annual shortage will probably reach mammoth proportions.[15]

In such a situation the competition for scarce grain would be bitter. The result could easily be a terrible global conflict. Like it or not, North Americans and Australians would have to decide who received the scarce grain. And we would select who lived or died either on the basis of narrow political self-interest or a moral commitment to the good of all.

A new food policy *now* is one way to avoid such a dangerous situation. The constantly growing demand for food must stop —or at least slow down dramatically. That means reduced affluence in the rich nations and population control everywhere. (Equally important, of course, is increased food production in the developing nations, which will be discussed later in this chapter.)

Norway has proved that a national food policy can make a difference. Aware of world food scarcity and concerned with increasing heart disease, the government decided to act. A few years ago they asked the medical profession to develop an optimum diet for Norwegians. In light of these recommendations, they then designed a national food policy to produce a desirable amount of wheat, milk, meat and so on. They used public education programmes and economic incentives to encourage people to produce and use lean meat instead of fattier grain-fed meat. Increased direct consumption of grain and vegetables permitted less reliance on livestock products and sugar. The result has been threefold: improved health and life expectancy; a lower agricultural trade deficit; and a reduced demand on the world's limited supply of land, water and fertilizer.[16]

All other industrialized nations—especially the United States, Canada and Western Europe—should do the same. In the end the only solution to world hunger is drastically reduced population growth and increased food production in poor countries. But in the short run, affluent nations must consume less so that they can export more. Professor Jean Mayer of Harvard University has estimated that a ten per cent reduction of meat consumption in North America "would release enough grain to feed 60 million people".[17]

If meat consumption dropped, the demand for corn would fall. But that would not be a problem, according to Dr. Folke Dovring, an agricultural economist at the University of Illinois. It is not difficult to switch land from corn to wheat and soya beans (and they take less fertilizer too!).[18] Some land, obviously, is only suitable for grazing. But much more of the land which can grow grain for direct consumption should be used for that purpose. It will require a national policy decision to accomplish this transition.

If the United States, Canada and Australia would adopt this kind of food policy, what should they do with the extra grain? The World Food Conference's call for world food reserves should be implemented immediately. If international trade patterns are changed as outlined earlier in the chapter, some food-deficit countries will be able to purchase more grain. Others will need outright gifts *in the short term*, especially during the likely emergencies in the next two decades. In recent years much of the food assistance has been in terms of loans, not grants. As a result, in 1974 payments to the U.S. government for previous food assistance loans *exceeded* the U.S.'s new help by $174 million.[19] More outright grants are essential.

We must be sure, however, that these grants do not discourage grain production or permit the postponement of necessary agricultural reforms in the developing countries themselves. To avoid the former, donated grain can be used in "food-for-work" projects where food is used to pay the labourers. These projects should promote rural agricultural development, thereby contributing to a long-term solution. To make sure that food aid does not encourage countries to postpone hard political decisions on necessary agricultural reforms, especially land redistribution and population control programmes, the United States and Canada should announce that food aid will go only to the countries which are implementing the internationally agreed upon world plan of action drawn up at the U.N.'s Population Conference (Bucharest, 1974) and the U.N.'s World Food Conference (Rome, 1974).[20]

A new food programme must be clearly designed for humanitarian rather than political purposes. In 1974 fully one-half of all U.S. food aid went, for obvious political reasons, to the two tiny countries of South Vietnam and Cambodia. Even under recent legislation the government can grant 25 per cent of total food aid to countries not on the internationally accepted list of MSA (Most Seriously Affected) countries. In 1976 the lion's share of this unrestricted 25 per cent went to Chile and South Korea.[21] Both countries have repressive dictatorships. And both are among the richest of the developing countries! The political misuse of food aid could be largely avoided if food assistance went through U.N. channels and private charitable organizations rather than via agreements between the United States and individual developing nations.

We have only sketched the barest outlines of a new food policy. A plan of this sort would seem to represent a concrete application of the biblical principle that persons and nations are stewards, not absolute owners, of their resources. The human right to a just living transcends the right of North Americans to use their vast grain fields solely for themselves.

The plan sketched here could become national policy in the industrialized nations. But that will happen only if a creative minority gives sacrificially of their time to change public policy.

GIVE BOMBS OR BREAD? Between 1947 and 1952, the United States poured $23 billion ($47 billion worth in terms of 1975 dollars) into Western Europe under the Marshall Plan.[22] One only has to look at the material prosperity of Western Europe today to realise that it was the most successful aid programme the world has ever seen. The plight of one billion poor people is just as desperate today, as that of the people of war-ravaged Europe in the late 1940's. The developed World, led by committed Christians in those countries, must lead the fight for greater trade and aid for the developing world.

Fortunately a new consensus on development assistance has recently emerged.[23] In the past, development theorists aimed at urban, capital-intensive, industrial development based on sophisticated technology. Rapid economic growth would allegedly have a trickle-down effect on the rural masses. But it did not happen. Today almost all development specialists agree that the emphasis must be reversed. The focus must be on improving the lot of the impoverished rural masses through labour-intensive methods and the use of appropriate technology.

From the World Food Conference to the World Bank, most people agree that the central emphasis must be on integrated rural development. The only long-term solution to hunger and malnutrition in the Third World is increased agricultural productivity there. That will mean land reform; agricultural extension services including credit, improved seeds, fertilizer, pesticides; rural public works programmes such as irrigation projects; and agricultural research.

It is particularly important that basic, minimal health care, education and a secure food supply be available to the rural masses.[24] Only then will the population explosion slow down. A recent study by the World Bank concludes:

In all developing countries, policies which succeed in improving the conditions of life for the poor, and in providing education and employment opportunities for women, are likely to reduce fertility. An improvement in the welfare of the poor appears to be essential before fertility can fall to developed country levels.[25]

Such a conclusion should not surprise the Christian. If, as the Bible teaches, God is at work in history liberating the poor and oppressed, then we should expect that an effective development strategy would be one that brings justice to the poor masses. At the same time the new approach to development provides a decisive answer to "lifeboat" theorists. Foreign aid to promote rural development is not a foolish gesture which sustains millions now only to doom even more later. Rather, foreign aid which encourages agricultural production as well as (at the least) minimal education and health care among the rural masses is probably the only way to check the population explosion in time to avoid global disaster. Justice and effectiveness coincide.

To implement the new strategy of rural development, increased foreign aid is imperative. Many of the developing countries simply do not have the resources to train the needed extension workers, undertake the necessary agricultural research, and perform other essential tasks. If the changes are to be implemented in time to avoid a runaway population explosion and widespread hunger, outside help is essential.

The World Food Congress (1974) recommended that $20 billion be spent on rural development annually. Three-fourths of this total, it suggested, should come from the poor countries themselves. The rich world need provide only $5 billion a year in development assistance. But yet many Western countries have cut their aid programmes in response to their economic problems in 1974–76.

There should also be changes in the way foreign aid is given.

Development assistance must be clearly separated from military assistance. We should not give development assistance on the basis of short-term political considerations. Aid should flow through international channels especially the United Nations. Internationally recognized standards for development assistance would be extremely valuable. Arthur Simon, director of Bread for the World, suggests a few:

The standards would include: (a) need; (b) evidence that development is occurring among the masses of poor people; (c) evidence of basic reforms, such as land reform, tax reform, and anticorruption measures, in order to reduce the disparity between rich and poor within a country; (d) efforts to secure human rights; and (e) de-emphasis on military spending.[26]

The adherence to standards of this kind should determine how much assistance countries receive.

The world faces a crucial choice. The next steps to help the poor and hungry on the scale needed require enormous sums of money. Tragically, the governments of the world continue to prefer bombs to bread. World expenditures on armaments spiral upward each year. Do the people of the world want to spend as much on arms each year (about $300 billion in 1976) as the poorest half of humanity receives in total annual income? President Eisenhower was surely correct: "Every gun that is made, every warship launched, every rocket fired signifies, in the final sense, a theft from those who hunger and are not fed, those who are cold and are not clothed."[27]

There are many other proposals for promoting development in the Third World. Changes are needed in the International Monetary Fund.[28] Some have suggested a system of international taxation. A tax on the consumption of nonrenewable resources could provide income for development in poor nations. Others have proposed putting under U.N. control all areas of the world not now controlled by individual nations: the oceans and the ocean floor, air space above the oceans, and outer space. Taxes could be levied on ships, aeroplanes and telecommunications. The mineral and other wealth of the oceans and Antarctica could be tapped to provide an additional source of funding for development.

The tasks outlined in this chapter seem overwhelming. Only as individuals join with other concerned citizens can they effectively promote the necessary structural changes. Here are a few organizations working to change public policy.

BREAD FOR THE WORLD Bread for the World (BFW) is a Christian citizens' movement in the United States whose goal is to change governmental policy on all issues that affect hungry people. BFW has not established a professional lobby in Washington. Instead it is organizing local chapters at the grassroots level in every Congressional district across the country. A monthly newsletter keeps members up to date on current administrative and legislative activity. Members influence legislation by calling, writing or visiting government officials, especially their own Congressional representatives.

Bread for the World is an explicitly Christian organization. Worship is a regular part of the meetings of local chapters. Art Simon, the director, is a devout Missouri Synod Lutheran. Christians from a wide range of denominations participate. A number of well-known evangelicals are active on the Board of Directors: Paul Rees, vice president of World Vision; Frank Gaebelein, former co-editor of *Christianity Today*; Owen Cooper, former president of the Southern Baptist Convention; Tom Skinner a black evangelist based in New York; and Senator Mark Hatfield.

Bread for the World practises what it preaches. Salaries are based primarily on need, not position. The Director manages to live (in New York City) on $8,400! Volunteers carry out most of BFW's activities, and income comes largely from the $10 annual membership fee.

Founded in 1974, BFW is a rapidly growing movement. Membership in early 1978 was approximately twenty thousand. It has already affected public policy. BFW's offering of letters which were sent to Congress after Thanksgiving 1975 attracted widespread attention for the "Right to Food" resolution submitted in the House and Senate. This resolution would declare that it is the sense of the U.S. Congress that "every person in this country and throughout the world has the right to food—the right to a nutritionally adequate diet—and that this right is henceforth to be recognized as a cornerstone of U.S. policy."

Bread for the World offers Christian citizens an effective way to help shape the public policies which will mean life or death for millions of people in the next few decades. (For information, write to: Bread for the World, 207 East 16th St., New York, N.Y. 10003.)

There are numerous other organizations attempting to change public policy. The following are among the more important.

The Interreligious Taskforce on U.S. Food Policy is a Washington-based religious lobby. It consists of the Washington staff of U.S. religious bodies. The staff analyzes issues, testifies before Congress and monitors legislation on all hunger related matters. The Taskforce mails a regular newsletter, an occasional newsletter called *Hunger*, and appeals for urgent communication with members of Congress when food legislation is pending. (To join, write to 110 Maryland Ave., N.E., Washington, D.C. 20002.)

The Interfaith Centre on Corporate Responsibility has a major emphasis on the relation of multinational corporations to world hunger. One-sixth of the total Gross World Product is controlled by multinational corporations. In fact, the combined annual sales of the five largest multinational corporations exceed the GNP of all but the four richest countries. Hence a concern for public policy necessarily extends to the activities of multinational corporations.[29] Although not a membership organization, the Interfaith Centre provides information on request. (Write to: National Council of Churches, 475 Riverside Dr., New York, N.Y. 10027.)

Other citizen lobbies include: Network, an organization staffed by Catholic sisters who publish a monthly newsletter, a quarterly, and a hunger packet (224 D St., S.E., Washington, D.C. 20005); and Friends Committee on National Legislation which also issues a monthly newsletter (245 Second St., N.E., Washington, D.C. 20002).

Details of British organizations concerned with development can be found on p. 219.

The proposals suggested thus far envisage the reform of present economic structures. An increasing number of biblical Christians, however, are beginning to call for even more sweeping structural change.[30] Careful examination of this growing debate, however, would carry us beyond both the space limitations of this chapter and the author's competence. Still, it is increasingly clear that it is time to re-examine economic orthodoxies of all ideological perspectives.

We desperately need economists deeply immersed in biblical faith who will fundamentally rethink economics as if poor people mattered. I have only an incomplete idea of what a modern version of the year of Jubilee would look like. But at the heart of God's call for Jubilee is a divine demand for regular, fundamental redistribution of the means for producing wealth. We must discover new, concrete models for applying this biblical principle in our global village. I hope and pray for a new generation of economists and political scientists who will devote their lives to formulating, developing and implementing a contemporary model of Jubilee.

The Liberty Bell which was made in Great Britain and now hangs in historic Philadelphia could become a powerful symbol for Western citizens working to share our resources with the poor of the world. The inscription on the Liberty Bell, "Proclaim liberty throughout the land", comes from the biblical passage on Jubilee (Lev. 25:10)! These words promised freedom and land to earn a living to Hebrews enslaved in debt. Today poverty enslaves hundreds of millions. The God of the Bible still demands institutionalized mechanisms which enable everyone to earn a just living. The Jubilee inscription on the Liberty Bell issues a ringing call for international economic justice. Do Christians have the courage to demand and implement the structural changes needed to make that ancient inscription a contemporary reality?

Epilogue

We live at one of the great turning points in history. The present division of the world's resources dare not continue. And it will not. Either courageous pioneers will persuade reluctant nations to share the good earth's bounty or we will enter an era of catastrophic conflict.

Christians should be in the vanguard. The church of Jesus Christ is the most universal body in the world today. All we need to do is truly obey the One we rightly worship. But to obey will mean to follow. And he lives among the poor and oppressed, seeking justice for those in agony. In our time, following in his steps will mean simple personal lifestyles. It will mean transformed churches with a corporate lifestyle consistent with worship of the God of the poor. It will mean costly commitment to structural change in secular society.

Do Christians today have that kind of faith and courage? Will we pioneer new models of sharing for our global village? Will we dare to become the vanguard in the struggle for structural change?

Sadly I must confess my fear that the majority of affluent "Christians" of all theological labels have bowed the knee to Mammon. If forced to choose between defending their luxuries and following Jesus among the oppressed, I am afraid they will imitate the rich young ruler.

But still I am not pessimistic! God regularly accomplishes his will through faithful remnants. Even in affluent nations, there are millions and millions of Christians who love their Lord Jesus more than houses and lands. More and more Christians are coming to realize that their Lord calls them to feed the hungry and seek justice for the oppressed.

If at this moment in history a few million Christians in

affluent nations dare to join hands with the poor around the world, we will decisively influence the course of world history. Together we must strive to be a biblical people ready to follow wherever Scripture leads. We must pray for the courage to bear any cross, suffer any loss and joyfully embrace any sacrifice that biblical faith requires in an Age of Hunger.

We know that our Lord Jesus is alive! We know that the decisive victory over sin and death has occurred. We know that the Sovereign of the universe wills an end to hunger, injustice and oppression. The resurrection of Jesus is our guarantee that in spite of the massive evil that sometimes almost overwhelms us, the final victory will surely come.[1] Secure on that solid rock, we will plunge into this unjust world, changing now all we can and knowing that the Risen King will complete the victory at his glorious return.

Notes

PART ONE

CHAPTER 1

1. "Iracema's Story," *Christian Century*, Nov. 12, 1975, p. 1030.

2. Robert L. Heilbroner, *The Great Ascent: The Struggle for Economic Development in Our Time* (New York: Harper & Row, 1963), pp. 33–36.

3. National Research Council, *World Food and Nutrition Study: The Potential Contributions of Research* (Washington: National Academy of Sciences, 1977), p. 34.

4. United Nations World Food Conference. Assessment of the World Food situation present and future, Rome 1974, pp. 55–73. E/Conf 65/3. For a description of the methodology used see pp. 65–66, 70–73. A useful summary of pp. 55–73 can be found in "The State of Food and Agriculture 1975" – pp. 75–77. Food and Agriculture Organization of the United Nations, Rome 1976.

5. 1974 Production year book of the F.A.O. Rome 1975, pp. 29–30.

6. See James W. Howe *et al.*, *The U.S. and World Development: Agenda for Action*, 1975 (New York: Praeger, 1975), pp. 35–39, 198–201.

7. Arthur Simon, *Bread for the World* (Grand Rapids: Eerdmans: Paramus, NJ: Paulist Press, 1975), pp. 64–65. *The New York Times* reported on July 11, 1976, F,3: "According to (Brazilian) government statistics, wages for unskilled workers, after taking inflation into account, have fallen almost 40 per cent since the right-wing military government took power 12 years ago. Meanwhile the Gross National Product rose more than 150 per cent in the period . . . There has been a radical distribution of income in favour of wealthier economic sectors." Also:

"Brazil's agriculture expands fast, but mostly for benefit of well-to-do." *New York Times*, August 16, 1976, p. 2.

8. H. Shenery *et al.*, *Redistribution with Growth* (Oxford University Press, 1974), p. 8.

9. Theodore Morgan, *Economic Development: Concept and Strategy* (New York: Harper, 1976), p. 205. See pp. 167–190 of Morgan for an excellent overview of the effects of malnutrition.

10. Robert McNamara (President of World Bank), *One Hundred Countries, Two Billion People* (Praeger, 1973), p. 103.

11. W. Stanley Mooneyham, *What Do You Say to a Hungry World?* (Waco, Texas: Word Books, 1975), pp. 38–39. Used by permission of Word Books, Publisher, Waco, Texas.

12. 1974 Production year book of the F.A.O. Rome 1975, pp. 25–26, 29–30.

13. John W. Sewell *et al.*, *United States and World Development. Agenda 1977* (Praeger, London), p. 188. Calculations from this table show that 1972–1974 price of Nitrogenous Fertilizer rose by 230 per cent. Phosphate rose by 127 per cent. Potash by 40 per cent. Weighted average price rise is 150 per cent. See also State of Food and Agriculture 1975, pp. 26–30.

14. "Food prospects: Better, But not for long," *Development Forum*, U.N. (Jan–Feb, 1977), p. 1.

15. Larry Minear, *New Hope for the Hungry?* (New York: Friendship Press, 1975), p. 50

16. Lester R. Brown, *In the Human Interest* (Oxford: Pergamon Press, 1976).

17. Minear, *New Hope for the Hungry?* p. 19.

18. Ruth Rice Puffer and Carlo V. Serrano, *Patterns of Mortality in childhood: Report of the Inter-American investigation of mortality in Childhood*. World Health Organization, Pan American health organizations, scientific publication No. 262, Washington D.C. 1973, pp. 164–66.

19. *Child of the Dark: The Diary of Carolina Maria de Jesus* (New York: Dutton, 1962), p. 42.

20. Mooneyham, p. 48.

21. Brown, *In the Human Interest*.

22. *Ibid.*

23. Mooneyham, p. 191.

24. Quoted in *Bread for the World Newsletter*, July 1976. This issue has an excellent refutation of Hardin's and Paddock's call for triage and lifeboat ethics.

25. Donella H. Meadows *et al.*, *The Limits to Growth*, 2nd ed. (New York: Universe Books, 1974).

26. Ervin Laszlo *et al.*, eds., *Goals for Mankind* (New York: Dutton, 1977); D. Gabor, *et al.*, eds., *Beyond The Age of Waste* (Elmsford, New York: Pergamon Press, 1978); Wassily Leontief *et al.*, *The Future of the World Economy*. A United Nations Study (Oxford University Press, 1977).

This computer project headed by U.S. economist (and Nobel Prize-winner) Professor Wassily Leontief concludes that there are adequate resources for continued economic growth in all nations for the foreseeable future.

27. Robert L. Heilbroner, *An Inquiry into the Human Prospect* (London: Calder, 1975).

28. *Ibid.*

29. Mooneyham, p. 50.

30. *World Hunger*, World Vision, XIX (February, 1975), p.5.

31. *Philadelphia Inquirer*, October 13, 1974, p. 9B.

32. Supplement to *Radar News*, January 1975, pp. 3–4.

33. Cf. Ronald J. Sider, "Where Have All the Liberals Gone?" *The Other Side*, May–June, 1976, pp. 42–44; *Shaft*, No. 14, December 1976.

CHAPTER 2

1. *Revolution through Peace* (New York: Harper & Row, 1971), p. 142.

2. Howe, p. 166.

3. *Newsweek*, August 18, 1975, p. 66. Irving B. Kravis, *et al.*, *A System of International Comparisons of Gross Product and Purchasing Power* (Baltimore: Johns Hopkins University Press, 1975), especially pp. 8–9.

4. John W. Sewell *et al.*, *U.S. and World Development Agenda 77* (Praeger, London), p. 170. For explanation of Physical Quality of Life Index see pp. 147–52. The main problems with using this index as a measurement of development in developing countries, is the unreliability of the data, of all three statistics used, which may be based on a small sample, and in the case of some countries, the latest data available is over 20 years old.

5. Howe, p. 209.

6. *Bread for the World Newsletter*, January, 1975, p. 2; and personal conversation with George Allen, U.S. Department of Agriculture on April 9, 1976.

7. "Facts on Food," Supplement to *Development Forum*, Nov., 1974.

8. "Malnutrition and Hunger in the United States," *American Medical Journal*, 213, No. 2 (1970), pp. 272–75.

9. *New York Times*, July 12, 1949. Quoted in Jules Henry, *Culture Against Man* (New York: Random House, 1963), p. 19.

10. Calculated on the basis of average television viewing of about 20 hours per week, of which half is I.T.V. and half B.B.C. (1 & 2). Commercial time is limited to a maximum of six minutes per hour, so about 10–20 commercials per hour on average may be watched.

11. Richard K. Taylor, "The Imperative of Economic De-Development," *The Other Side*, July–August, 1974, p. 17. The spending on advertising in the U.K. is from the Advertising Association.

12. Robert N. Bellah, *The Broken Covenant* (New York: Seabury Press, 1975), p. 134. See also Wilbur Schramm, Jack Lyle and Edwin N. Parker, *Television in the Lives of Our Children* (Stanford: Stanford University Press, 1961).

13. John V. Taylor, *Enough is Enough* (London: SCM Press, 1975), p. 71.

14. Patrick Kerans, *Sinful Social Structures* (New York: Paulist Press, 1974), pp. 80–81.

15. See the helpful comments on this in Art Gish, *Beyond the Rat Race* (Scottdale, Pa.: Herald Press, 1973), pp. 122–26.

16. Quoted in a supplement to the U.N. *Development Forum*, April, 1976, p. 2 (my italics).

17. Any system used to allocate a scarce commodity, such as medical help or food, only to those whom it may help to survive and not to those who have no chance of surviving or who will survive without assistance.

18. Garrett Hardin, "Lifeboat Ethics: The Case Against Helping the Poor", *Psychology Today*, 8, No. 4 (Sept. 1974), pp. 38ff. See also William and Paul Paddock, *Famine 1975!* (Boston: Little, Brown and Co. 1967). (Reprinted in 1976 under the title *Time of Famines: America and the World Food Crisis*.)

19. Brown, *In the Human Interest* (my italics).

20. Labour-intensive development uses people rather than machines (e.g. dams can be built by 5000 people carrying ground and stones just as well as by two bulldozers and three earth-movers). Advocates of intermediate technology urge developing nations to move from, for example, the hoe to the ox-drawn plough rather than from the hoe to the huge tractor. See E. F. Schumacher, *Small Is Beautiful* (London: Sphere, 1974).

21. Howe, *Agenda for Action*, 1975, pp. 60–62.

22. For short critiques of triage and lifeboat ethics, see Lester

Brown, *The Politics and Responsibility of the North-American Breadbasket*, p. 36; and *Bread for the World Newsletter*, July, 1976.

PART TWO

1. Quoted in *Post-American*, I, No. 4 (Summer 1972), p. 1.
2. Laudicina, *World Poverty and Development*, p. 78.

CHAPTER 3

1. See for instance Enzo Gatti, *Rich Church–Poor Church?* (Maryknoll: Orbis, 1974), p. 43.
2. Unlike some Liberation Theologians who take the Exodus merely as an inspirational device, I assert that in the Exodus, God was *both* liberating oppressed persons and *also* calling out a special people to be the recipients of his special revelation. Yahweh called forth a special people so that through them he could reveal his will and salvation for all people. But his will included, as he revealed ever more clearly to his covenant people, the fact that his people should follow him and be on the side of the poor and oppressed. The fact that Yahweh did not liberate all poor Egyptians at the Exodus does not mean that he was not concerned for the poor everywhere any more than the fact that he did not give the Ten Commandments to everyone in the Near East means that he did not intend them to have universal application. Because God chose to reveal himself in history, he disclosed to particular people at particular points in time what he willed for all people everywhere.
3. John Bright, *A History of Israel* (London: SCM Press, 1972)
4. *Ibid.*
5. Roland de Vaux, *Ancient Israel* (London: Darton, Longman & Todd, 1973), II, 72–73.
6. So also in the case of Judah; cf. Ezekiel 20, Jeremiah 11: 9–10.
7. Preaching the Gospel and seeking justice for the poor are *distinct, equally important* dimensions of the total mission of the church; see my "Evangelism, Salvation and Social Justice: Definitions and Interrelationships," *International Review of Mission*, July, 1975, pp. 251ff (especially p. 258), and my "Evangelism or Social Justice: Eliminating the Options," *Christianity Today*, 8 October 1976, pp. 26–29.

8. See also the discussion of Exodus 20:2 above, p. 55, and Revelation 7:16.

9. Luke 2:24. Cf. Leviticus 12:6–8.

10. Richard Batey, *Jesus and the Poor* (New York: Harper, 1972), p. 7.

11. Martin Hengel, *Property and Riches in the Early Church: Aspects of a Social History of Early Christianity* (London: SCM Press, 1974).

12. Batey, *Jesus and the Poor*, p. 6.

13. See also Psalm 107:35–41. See below, pp. 115–16, for a discussion of the different versions of the beatitudes in Matthew 5 and Luke 6.

14. One dare not overlook, of course, the biblical teaching that obedience brings prosperity. See above, pp. 113–14 for a discussion of this theme.

15. Bright, *History of Israel*. For a similar event, see Daniel 4 (especially verse 27).

16. See above, pp. 55–58; see also Micah 2:1–3.

17. Joachim Jeremias, *The Parables of Jesus* (London, 1954), pp. 128–30, and others have argued that Jesus' point was an entirely different one. But I am still inclined to follow the usual interpretation; see for instance, *The Interpreter's Bible*, 8, 288–92.

18. *Ibid.*, p. 290.

19. Clark H. Pinnock, "An Evangelical Theology of Human Liberation," *Sojourners*, Feb. 1976, p. 31.

20. Cf. also Isaiah 1:10–17.

21. "The Bible and the Other Side," *The Other Side*, 11, No. 5 (Sept.–Oct., 1975), p. 57.

22. See also Hebrews 13:1–3.

23. See J. A. Moyter, *The Day of the Lion: The Message of Amos* (London: Inter-Varsity, 1974), for a good exegesis of these verses. See also Micah 6:6–8; James 2:14–17.

24. That is not to say that God is unconcerned with true worship. Nor does Amos 5:21–24 mean: "I do not want you to defend my rights, real or imaginary; I want you to struggle and expend your energies in advancing the rights of the poor and oppressed." (Gatti, *Rich Church–Poor Church?*, p. 17.) Such a dichotomy ignores the central prophetic attack on idolatry. God wants both worship and justice. Tragically, some people today concentrate on one, some on the other. Few seek both simultaneously.

25. George E. Ladd, *A Theology of the New Testament* (Guildford: Lutterworth Press, 1975), p. 133.

26. Nor does God desire the salvation of the poor more than the salvation of the rich. I disagree strongly with Gatti's assertion: "They [the poor and oppressed] are the ones that have the best right to that word; they are the privileged recipients of the Gospel" (*Rich Church–Poor Church?*, p. 43). God desires all people—oppressors and oppressed alike—to be saved. No one has any "right" to hear God's Word. We all deserve death. It is only by contrast with the sinful perversity of Christians who prefer to preach in the suburbs rather than the slums that Jesus and Paul seem to be biased in favour of preaching to the poor.

27. See chapter 6, pp. 120–125.

CHAPTER 4

1. See in this connection the fine article by Paul G. Schrotenboer, "The Return of Jubilee," *International Reformed Bulletin*, Fall, 1973, pp. 19ff (especially pp. 23–24).

2. See also Ephesians 2:13–17. Marc H. Tanenbaum points out the significance of the day of atonement in "Holy Year 1975 and its Origins in the Jewish Jubilee Year", *Jubilaeum* (1974), p. 64.

3. For the meaning of the word "liberty" in verse 10, see Martin Noth, *Leviticus* (Philadelphia: Westminster, 1965), p. 187: "derōr, a 'liberation' . . . is a feudal word from the Accadian (an)durāru = 'freeing from burdens'."

4. Roland de Vaux reflects the scholarly consensus that Leviticus 25 "was a Utopian law and it remained a dead letter". *Ancient Israel*, I, 177. Tanenbaum (*loc. cit.*, pp. 75–76) on the other hand, thinks it was practised. The only other certain references to it are in Leviticus 27:16–25, Numbers 36:4 and Ezekiel 46: 17. It would be exceedingly significant if one could show that Isaiah 61:1–2 (which Jesus cited to outline his mission in Luke 4:18–19) also refers to the year of Jubilee. De Vaux doubts that Isaiah 61:1 refers to the Jubilee (*Ancient Israel*, I, 176). The same word, however, is used in Isaiah 61:1 and Leviticus 25:10. See John H. Yoder's argument in *Politics of Jesus* (Grand Rapids: Eerdmans, 1972), pp. 64ff.

5. De Vaux, *Ancient Israel*, I, 173–75.

6. Leviticus 25 seems to provide for emancipation of slaves only every fiftieth year. But the purpose is the same: prevention of ever greater inequality among God's people.

7. See Jeremiah 34 for a fascinating account of God's anger at Israel for their failure to obey this command.

8. Some modern commentators think that Deuteronomy 15:1–11 provides for a one-year suspension of repayment of loans rather than an outright remission of them. See S. R. Driver, *Deuteronomy* (ICC; 3rd ed.; Edinburgh: T and T. Clark, 1895), pp. 179–80. But Driver's argument is basically that remission would have been *impractical*. He admits that verse 9 seems to point toward remission of loans. So too Gerhard von Rad, *Deuteronomy* (London: SCM Press, 1966).

9. See de Vaux, *Ancient Israel*, I, 174–75 for discussion of the law's implementation. In the Hellenistic period, there is clear evidence that it was put into effect.

10. See also de Vaux, *Ancient Israel*, I, 165.

11. This is an extremely complicated problem which has been debated throughout church history. The long dispute among Lutherans over the "third use of the law" is one example of the perennial debate.

12. De Vaux, *Ancient Israel*, I, 171.

13. See de Vaux, *op cit.*, p. 170; and Taylor, *Enough Is Enough*, pp. 56–60.

14. Driver, *Deuteronomy*, p. 178.

15. For a highly fascinating, scholarly account of the entire history, see Benjamin Nelson, *The Idea of Usury: From Tribal Brotherhood to Universal Otherhood*, 2nd ed. (Chicago: University of Chicago Press, 1969).

16. See Mark 1:14–15; Matthew 4:23; 24:14; Luke 4:43; 16:16; and my "Evangelism, Salvation and Social Justice", *International Review of Mission*, July, 1975, pp. 256ff.

17. For this common interpretation, see Batey, *Jesus and the Poor*, pp. 3, 9, 100, n.8; Ziesler, *Christian Asceticism*, p. 45; *TWNT*, *III*, 796; *Interpreter's Bible*, VIII, 655, 690; Carl Henry, "Christian Perspective on Private Property", *God and the Good*, ed. C. Orlebeke and L. Smedes (Grand Rapids: Eerdmans, 1975), p. 98.

18. See also Batey, *Jesus and the Poor* (New York: Harper, 1972), p. 8.

19. Taylor, *Economics and the Gospel* (Philadelphia: United Church Press, 1973), p. 21.

20. See above, p. 82.

21. See D. Guthrie, *et al.*, ed., *The New Bible Commentary Revised* (Leicester: Inter-Varsity Press, 1970); Batey, *Jesus and the Poor*, p. 38.

22. *TWNT, III,* 796.

23. The key verbs are *èpípraskon* and *diemérizon* (Acts 2:45) and *èpheron* (Acts 4:34). See *Interpreter's Bible, IX,* 52; Batey, *Jesus and the Poor,* pp. 33, 103, n.9.

24. Ziesler, *Christian Asceticism,* p. 110.

25. Batey, *Jesus and the Poor,* pp. 36, 96.

26. *Ibid.,* p. 36.

27. *Ibid.,* pp. 36, 96–97.

28. See Keith F. Nickle, *The Collection: A Study of Paul's Strategy,* "Studies in Biblical Theology", No. 48 (Naperville: Allenson, 1966), p. 29; and *Interpreter's Bible, IX,* 153.

29. See Diane Macdonald, "The Shared Life of the Acts Community", *Post-American,* July, 1975, p. 28.

30. See *Interpreter's Bible, IX,* 150–52 for a summary of the reasons for accepting the reliability of this account.

31. See Nickle, *The Collection,* pp. 68–69.

32. See *TWNT, III,* 804ff.

33. In fact, Paul was probably at Jerusalem to deliver the gift mentioned in Acts 11:27–30. See *Interpreter's Bible, IX,* 151.

34. See *TWNT, III,* 807–08.

35. See also the striking use of *koinonós* in Philemon 17ff. As fellow Christians, the slave Onesimus, his master Philemon and Paul are all partners (*koinonói*). This common fellowship means that Paul can ask Philemon to charge Onesimus's debt to his own account. But Paul and Philemon are also partners in Christ. Furthermore, Philemon owes Paul his very soul. Therefore, Paul suggests there is no need for anyone to reimburse Philemon. Their fellowship in Christ cancels any debt that Onesimus might otherwise owe! See *TWNT, III,* 807.

36. (The italics are mine.) Not all translations are accurate. But the Greek word *isótēs* clearly means "equality". So Charles Hodge: "The word *isótēs* means here neither reciprocity nor equity, but equality, as the illustration in verse 15 shows." *An Exposition of the Second Epistle to the Corinthians* (Edinburgh: Banner of Truth Trust, 1974). So too C. K. Barrett, *The Second Epistle to the Corinthians* (London: A. & C. Black, 1973); and the Inter-Varsity commentary by R. V. G. Tasker, *The Second Epistle of Paul to the Corinthians* (London: Tyndale Press, 1971).

37. Quoted in Hengel, *Property and Riches in the Early Church,* pp. 42–43.

38. *Ibid.,* pp. 42–44.

39. Ep. 84; quoted in *ibid.,* p. 45.

40. C. H. Jacquet, Jr., ed., *Yearbook of American and Canadian Churches: 1974* (New York: National Council of Churches, 1974), p. 263.

41. See Helmut Gollwitzer, *The Rich Christians and Poor Lazarus*, trans. David Cairns (Edinburgh: St Andrew Press, 1970), and Arthur C. Cochrane, *Eating and Drinking with Jesus* (Philadelphia: Westminster Press, 1974).

CHAPTER 5

1. So, correctly, Carl F. H. Henry, "Christian Perspective on Private Property", in *God and the Good*, ed. Clifton Orlebeke and Lewis Smedes (Grand Rapids: Eerdman's 1975), p. 97; Hengel, *Property and Riches in the Early Church*, p. 15.

2. See further Emil Brunner, *Justice and the Social Order*, trans. Mary Hottinger (London: Lutterworth Press, 1945), pp. 42ff., 133ff. and E. Clinton Gardner, *Biblical Faith and Social Ethics* (New York: Harper, 1960), pp. 285–91.

3. Adam Smith, *The Wealth of Nations* (Oxford: Oxford University Press, 1976).

4. Henry, "Christian Perspective on Private Property", p. 97.

5. Hengel, *Property and Riches in the Early Church*, p. 12.

6. Walther Eichrodt, "The Question of Property in the Light of the Old Testament", in *Biblical Authority for Today*, ed. Alan Richardson and W. Schweitzer (London: SCM Press, 1951), p. 261.

7. *Ibid.*, p. 271.

8. See further Gardner, *Biblical Faith and Social Ethics*, pp. 276–77.

9. *Interpreter's Bible, VII*, 320; see also 1 Timothy 6:17–19.

10. A. W. Argyle, *Matthew*, "The Cambridge Bible Commentary" (Cambridge: Cambridge University Press, 1963), p. 58. So too *Interpreter's Bible, VII*, 318.

11. Camara, *Revolution through Peace* (New York: Harper, 1971), pp. 142–43.

12. *TWNT, VI*, 271. Taylor (*Enough is Enough*, p. 45) suggests that the word connotes "excess" or "wanting more and more".

13. For a discussion of church discipline, see my "Watching Over One Another in Love", *The Other Side, XI* (May–June, 1975), 10ff (especially p. 59).

14. For a good discussion of this issue, see J. A. Ziesler, *Christian Asceticism* (Grand Rapids: Eerdmans, 1973).

15. See pp. 54–58, 64–69.

16. See further the twenty references in Batey, *Jesus and the Poor*, p. 92.

17. Ziesler. *Christian Asceticism*, p. 52.

18. See p. 31.

CHAPTER 6

1. See "Edison High School—A History of Benign and Malevolent Neglect", *The Oakes Newsletter*, V, No. 4 (Dec. 14, 1973), pp. 1–4; and "Northeast High Took the Glory Away", *The Sunday Bulletin*, Jan. 27, 1974, sect. 1, p. 3.

2. *Psychology Today*, April, 1970, pp. 38ff.

3. John Bright, *A History of Israel* (London: SCM Press, 1972).

4. Cf. also Isaiah 3:13–17.

5. Mooneyham, *Hungry World*, pp. 128, 117.

6. See especially Gheddo, *Why Is the Third World Poor?*

7. Paul A. Laudicina, *World Poverty and Development: A Survey of American Opinion* (Washington: Overseas Development Council, 1973), p. 51.

8. For a balanced summary, see Gheddo, *Why Is the Third World Poor?*, pp. 69ff.

9. Simon, *Bread for the World*, p. 41.

10. For a careful discussion of how U.S. tariff structures discriminate against the exports of poor countries, see Guy F. Erb, "U.S. Trade Policies Toward Developing Areas", *Columbia Journal of World Business*, VIII, No. 3 (Fall, 1973), pp. 59–67.

11. James P. Grant, "Can the Churches Promote Development?" *Ecumenical Review*, XXVI (Jan., 1974), p. 26.

12. Howe, *Agenda for Action*, 1975, p. 42.

13. Theodore Morgan, *Economic Development: Concept and Strategy* (New York: Harper, 1975), p. 316.

14. *New Internationalist*, August, 1975, p. 1.

15. Hans W. Singer, *International Development: Growth and Change* (New York: McGraw Hill, 1964), p. 165.

16. Unfortunately, much of that increased oil profit remained with the already wealthy elite in otherwise poor countries, profiting the average person very little. This problem is addressed in chapter 9, pp. 180–83.

17. See "A Study of the Problems of Raw Materials and Development", U.N. Document A/9556 (part II), May 1, 1974; and *Newsweek*, Sept. 15, 1975, pp. 38–40.

18. Grant, "Can the Churches Promote Development?" p. 26.

19. For a recent discussion of America's relation to Latin America, see the report prepared for the Board of Directors of the American Friends Service Committee: *The United States and Latin America Today* (Philadelphia: AFSC, 1976).

20. Brown, p. 92.

21. *Newsweek*, April 1, 1974, pp. 40–41.

22. E. F. Schumacher, "Implication of the Limits to Growth Debate—Small Is Beautiful", *Anticipation*, No. 13, Dec. 1972, p. 14 (WCC).

23. *Global Justice and Development* (Washington: Overseas Development Council, 1975), p. 15.

24. Lester R. Brown, *By Bread Alone* (Oxford: Pergamon Press, 1975).

25. F.A.O. Production year book – 1974, p. 42.

26. Simon, *Bread for the World*, pp. 19–20.

27. Borgstrom's mimeographed lecture, "Present Food Production and the World Food Crisis", presented on Sept 2nd, 1974, pp. 5–7.

28. The fact that Peru feels it must sell this protein needed by its hungry people in order to gain foreign exchange underlines the fact that complex, national and international social and political changes are necessary if the poor are to be fed adequately.

29. Georg Borgstrom, *The Food and People Dilemma* (Belmont, Calif.: Duxbury Press, 1973), p. 64.

30. Simon, *Bread for the World*, pp. 20, 25.

31. Borgstrom, "Present Food Production", p. 12.

32. Borgstrom, *The Food and People Dilemma*, pp. 63, 128.

33. Borgstrom, "Present Food Production . . .", p. 12.

34. *Ibid.*

35. Grant, "Can the Churches Promote Development?", p. 24.

36. Howe, *Agenda for Action, 1975*, pp. 212–13.

37. *New York Times*, July 22, 1975, p. 8.

38. *Ibid.*

39. Chapter 1, footnote 18.

40. U.S. Chamber of Commerce, *Survey of Current Business* (October, 1971), p. 35.

41. Simon, *Bread for the World*, p. 103.

42. Gunnar Myrdal, *The Challenge of World Poverty* (London: Penguin, 1970).

43. *Ibid.*, quoted on pp. 322–23.

44. Brown, *In the Human Interest*.

45. *Markings* (New York: Knopf, 1964), p. XXI.

46. *Philadelphia Inquirer*, April 10, 1975, pp. 1–2.

47. See "Bananas", *New Internationalist*, August, 1975, p. 2.

48. "Action", *New Internationalist*, August, 1975, p. 32.

49. Carl Oglesby and Richard Shaull, *Containment and Change* (New York: Macmillan, 1967), p. 104.

50. "America's World Role: Should We Feel Guilty?" *Philadelphia Inquirer*, July 18, 1974, p. 7A.

51. See the helpful comments on this in Patrick Kerans, *Sinful Social Structures* (New York: Paulist Press, 1974), pp. 47–51.

CHAPTER 7

1. Ronald J. Sider, ed., *The Chicago Declaration* (Carol Stream: Creation House, 1974), p. 2.

2. *Let the Earth Hear His Voice: International Congress on World Evangelization, Lausanne, Switzerland*, ed. by J. D. Douglas (Minneapolis: World Wide Publications, 1975), p. 6, section 9.

3. "Creation, Technology, and Human Survival", Plenary Address, WCC's Fifth Assembly, Dec. 1, 1975.

4. This sermon was one of the series of sermons which constituted the standard doctrines of the early Methodists. See *The Works of John Wesley* (London: Wesleyan Conference Office, 1872) [reprint by Zondervan], V, 361ff.

5. *Ibid.*, pp. 365–68.

6. J. Wesley Bready, *England: Before and After Wesley* (London: Hodder and Stoughton, n.d.), p. 238.

7. For an article based on the Wesley Principle applied practically to contemporary Britain, see "Enough is as Good as a Feast", *Third Way*, January 1979.

8. See Donella H. Meadows, *et al.*, *The Limits to Growth*, 2nd ed. (New York: Universe Books, 1974), p. 165.

9. Walter and Ginny Hearn, "The Price Is Right", *Right On*, May, 1973, pp. 1, 11. Used by permission of *Radix* (formerly *Right On*) of the Berkeley Christian Coalition.

10. *Ibid.*, p. 13.

11. Michael Harper, *A New Way of Living* (London: Hodder and Stoughton, 1974). The early leader of the church, W. Graham Pulkingham, has written two books about Church of the Redeemer: *Gathered for Power* (London: Hodder and Stoughton, 1973) and *They Left Their Nets* (London: Hodder and Stoughton, 1974).

11. Hearn, pp. 1, 11.

12. I owe a great deal to John F. Alexander in the development of these criteria.

13. For Christian organizations in the U.K., financing development programmes in the Third World, such as Tear Fund and Christian Aid, see Organizations, p. 219.

14. Minear, *New Hope for the Hungry*, p. 79.

CHAPTER 8

1. Dave and Neta Jackson, *Living Together in a World Falling Apart* (Carol Stream: Creation House, 1974), p. 15.

2. See above, chapter 4, pp. 88–97.

3. See my "Spare the Rod and Spoil the Church", *Eternity*, October, 1976, pp. 16ff.

4. From John Wesley's account (1743) of the origin of the class meetings. *The Works of John Wesley* (Grand Rapids: Zondervan, n.d.), VIII, 269.

5. Peter Berger, *A Rumour of Angels* (Harmondsworth: A. Lane, 1976). See also Peter Berger and Thomas Luckman, *The Social Construction of Reality* (Harmondsworth: A. Lane, 1967).

6. Berger, *A Rumour of Angels*, p. 17. See further pp. 41ff. for Berger's rejection of the common idea that the sociology of knowledge leads inexorably to thoroughgoing relativism.

7. See Floyd Filson, "The Significance of the Early House Churches", *Journal of Biblical Literature*, LVIII (1939), pp. 105–112. See also the brief overview in John W. Miller's (mimeographed) "House Church Handbook". For a copy, write to John Miller, Conrad Grebel College, University of Waterloo, Waterloo, Ont., Canada.

8. Personal conversation with John Poole. For further information and cassette tapes, write to Living Word Community, 142 N. 17th St., Philadelphia, Pa.

9. I have relied largely on Gordon Cosby's *Handbook for Mission Groups* (Waco, Texas: Word Books, 1975) for this discussion. See also Elizabeth O'Connor's several books about or for Church of the Saviour including: *Call to Commitment* (New York: Harper, 1963); *Journey Inward, Journey Outward* (New York: Harper, 1968).

10. Cosby, *Handbook for Mission Groups*, p. 63.

11. *Ibid.*, p. 140.

12. For further information about Dunamis and their regular

training institute, write to Dunamis, 203 C Street, N.E., Washington, D.C. 20002.

13. Howard A. Snyder, *New Wineskins: Church Structure in a Technological Age* (London: Marshall, Morgan & Scott, 1977).

14. For a discussion of Reba Place, see Dave and Neta Jackson *Living Together in a World Falling Apart*, especially pp. 36–39, 230–33. For the names and addresses of 24 communities, see pp. 287–97.

15. *Ibid.*, p. 183.

16. *Ibid.*, p. 65.

17. For a good historical perspective on Christian communes and an excellent bibliography, see Donald G. Bloesch, *Wellsprings of Renewal: Promise in Christian Communal Life* (Grand Rapids: Eerdmans, 1974). For a handbook by a Catholic charismatic, see Stephen B. Clark, *Building Christian Communities* (Notre Dame: Ave Maria Press, 1972).

CHAPTER 9

1. From an article in *Our Hope*, 10, No. 2 (August, 1903), pp. 76–77.

2. Galatians 6:16; 3:6–9; 1 Peter 2:9–10.

3. See Carl Oglesby and Richard Shaull, *Containment and Change* (New York: Macmillan, 1967), pp. 72–111.

4. See Amnesty International, *Report on Torture* (New York: Farrar, Straus, and Giroux, 1975), especially the special report on Chile on pp. 243ff. See also Fred B. Morris, "Sustained by Faith Under Brazilian Torture", *Christian Century*, Jan. 22, 1975, pp. 56–60; and *Latin America and Empire Report*, 10, No. 1 (Jan., 1976).

5. See especially President Carter's speech at the Roman Catholic University of Notre Dame in South Bend, Indiana on May 22nd, 1977. *The Times, Financial Times, Guardian* May 23rd, 1977, *Economist* May 28th, pp. 33–34.

6. "More help for the poorest" – Changing emphasis in British Aid Policies, Cmnd 6270, HMSO.

7. *The Times*, Sept. 19th, 1977, p. 17. See especially "Striking imbalance on size of loans to poorer countries".

8. Robert E. Frykenberg, ed., *Land Tenure and Peasant in South Asia: An Anthology of Recent Research* (Madison, Wisconsin: Land Tenure Center, 1976), p. 14.

9. Dom Helder Camara, *Revolution through Peace*, trans. Amparo McLean (New York: Harper, 1971), p. 92.

10. If the manifest tariff on goods is 10 per cent, and the inputs (raw materials etc) used in the production of the goods amount to 50 per cent of the value of production and these inputs are imported without duty, then the effective rate of protection accorded to the value added is 20 per cent, not 10 per cent as the manifest duty implies. This policy of charging tariffs on finished goods but allowing raw materials in without a tariff, leading to a high rate of effective protection is the policy of most developed countries as we saw earlier.

11. *Wall Street Journal*, Nov. 25, 1975, p. 3.

12. Hansen, *Agenda for Action 1976*, pp. 18–19.

13. Morgan, *Economic Development*, p. 320.

14. Lester R. Brown, *The Politics and Responsibility of the North American Breadbasket* (Worldwatch Paper, No. 2, Oct., 1975), p. 6.

15. C. Dean Freudenberger and Paul M. Minus, Jr., *Christian Responsibility in a Hungry World* (New York: Abingdon, 1976), p. 17.

16. Howe, *Agenda for Action, 1975*, pp. 79–80.

17. *Time*, Nov. 11, 1974, p. 67. Dr Kenneth Farrell, deputy director of the U.S. Department of Agriculture's Economic Research Service agrees that "in the long run, the argument [to cut meat consumption in order to feed more hungry people] is not without merit." *New York Times*, Nov. 28, 1974, p. 44.

18. *New York Times*. Nov. 28, 1974, p. 44.

19. Simon, *Bread for the World*, p. 116.

20. For a good discussion of the Rome Conference, see Minear, *New Hope for the Hungry*, pp. 52ff. For the Bucharest Conference, write to the United Nations, Center for Economic and Social Information, New York, N.Y. 10017.

21. *Hunger*, June, 1976, p. 3 (an occasional newsletter published by the Interreligious Taskforce on U.S. Food Policy, 100 Maryland Ave., Washington, D.C. 20002).

22. Simon, *Bread for the World*, p. 113.

23. For the following, see especially Howe, *Agenda for Action, 1975*, pp. 5, 157–88 (especially pp. 169–77); and Minear, *New Hope for the Hungry*, pp. 52ff.

24. See above, chapter 1, pp. 17–27.

25. Timothy King, ed., *Population Policies and Economic Development*, published for the World Bank (Baltimore: Johns Hopkins University Press, 1974), p. 54. See also William Rich,

Smaller Families Through Social and Economic Progress (Monograph, No. 7; Washington: Overseas Development Council, 1973), especially p. 76.

26. Simon, *Bread for the World*, p. 119.

27. *Ibid.*, p. 170.

28. See Guy F. Erb and Valeriana Kallab, *Beyond Dependency: The Developing World Speaks Out* (Washington: Overseas Development Council, 1975), pp. 160, 151.

29. See Richard J. Barnet and Ronald E. Müller, *Global Reach: The Power of the Multinational Corporations* (New York: Simon and Schuster, 1974); U.N. Department of Economic and Social Affairs, *Multinational Corporations in World Development* (1973) and *The Impact of Multinational Corporations in Development and International Affairs* (1974), both of which can be ordered from: United Nations Sales Section, U.N. Plaza, New York, N.Y. 10017.

30. See for instance *The Other Side*, Jan.–Feb. and March–April, 1976. For the possibility of applying the principles of nonviolent, direct action to the whole problem of world hunger and economic injustice, see Richard K. Taylor, "The Peacemakers", *Post American*, Oct.–Nov. 1975, pp. 16ff; and my Huston Memorial Peace Lecture, Bethany Theological Seminary (1975): "A Call for Evangelical Non-Violence", *Christian Century*, Sept. 15, 1976, pp. 753–57. Also Richard K. Taylor, *Blockade* (Maryknoll: Orbis, 1977).

EPILOGUE

1. See my "The Resurrection and Radical Discipleship", *Right On*, April, 1976, pp. 5ff, and "A Case for Easter", *HIS*, April, 1972, pp. 27–31. For a more extensive discussion, see also my "The Historian, the Miraculous and Post-Newtonian Man", *Scottish Journal of Theology*, XXV (1972), 309–19; "The Pauline Conception of the Resurrection Body in 1 Cor. 15:35–54", *New Testament Studies*, XXI (1975), 428–39; and my "St. Paul's Understanding of the Nature and Significance of the Resurrection in 1 Cor. 15:1–19", *Novum Testamentum*, XIX (1977), pp. 124–41.

Bibliography

Bauer, P. T. *Dissent on Development*. London: Weidenfeld and Nicolson, 1972.

Bhagwati, Jagdish and Eckaus, Richard S. *Foreign Aid*. London: Penguin, 1970.

Bhagwati, Jagdish. *The Economics of Underdeveloped Countries*. London: Weidenfeld and Nicolson, 1966.

Borgstrom, Georg. *World Food Resources*. Aylesbury, Bucks.: International Textbook Company, 1973.

Borgstrom, Georg. *The Food and People Dilemma*. North Scituate, Mass.: Duxbury Press, 1973.

Brown, Lester R. *In the Human Interest*. Oxford: Pergamon Press, 1976.

Brown, Michael B. *The Economics of Imperialism*. London: Penguin, 1974.

Cairncross, Sir Alec. *Factors in Economic Development*. London: Allen & Unwin, 1962.

Camara, Dom Helder. *Revolution Through Peace*. New York: Harper, 1971.

Chenery, Hollis B. (ed.). *Redistribution With Growth*. London: Oxford University Press, 1974.

Connelly, Philip and Perlman, Robert. *The Politics of Scarcity: Resource Conflicts in International Relations*. Oxford: Oxford University Press, 1975.

de Jesus, Carolina Maria. *Child of the Dark*. Trans. by David St. Clair. New York: Signet Books, c. 1962.

Dumont, René and Bernard, Rosier. *The Hungry Future*. London: Methuen, 1969.

Dunne, George H. *The Right to Development*. New York: Paulist Press, 1974.

Eckholm, Erik. *Losing Ground: Environmental Stress and World Food Prospects*. New York: Norton, 1976.

Elkan, Walter. *An Introduction to Development Economics*. London: Penguin, 1973.

Erb, Guy and Kallab, Valeriana. *Beyond Dependency: the Developing World Speaks Out*. New York: Praeger, 1976.

Freudenberger, C. Dean and Minus, Paul M. Jr. *Christian Responsibility in a Hungry World*. Nashville: Abingdon, 1976.

George, Susan. *How the Other Half Dies*. London: Penguin, 1976.

Gheddo, Piero. *Why is the Third World Poor?* Maryknoll, New York: Orbis Books, 1973.

Goulet, Denis. *A New Moral Order*. New York: Orbis Books, 1974.

Haq, Mahbub Ul. *The Poverty Curtain: Choices for the Third World*. Columbia, 1976.

Hawkins, Edward K. *Principles of Development Aid*. London: Penguin, 1970.

Hayter, Teresa. *Aid as Imperialism*. London: Penguin, 1971.

Heilbroner, Robert L. *An Inquiry into the Human Prospect*. London: Calder, 1975.

Huges, Helen (ed.) *Prospects for Partnership*. Baltimore: Johns Hopkins University Press, for the World Bank, 1973.

Johnson, Harry G. (ed.). *Trade Strategy for Rich and Poor Nations*. London: Allen & Unwin, for the Trade Policy Research Centre, 1971.

Johnson, Harry G. *Economic Policies Towards Less Developed Countries*. London: Allen & Unwin, 1968.

Lewis, Sir Arthur. *Theory of Economic Growth*. London: Allen & Unwin, 1955.

Lipton, Michael. *Why Poor People Stay Poor: Urban Bias in World Development*. London: Maurice Temple Smith, 1976.

Lissner, Jorgen. *The Politics of Altruism*, a study of political behaviour of voluntary development agencies. Geneva: Lutheran World Federation, 1977.

Macbean, Alastair I. and Balasubrananyam, V. N. *Meeting the Third World Challenge*. 2nd ed. London: Macmillan, for the Trade Policy Research Centre, 1978.

Mason, Edward S. and Asher, R. E. *The World Bank Since Bretton Woods*. Washington: Brookings Institution, 1973.

Matin, K. M. *The Bargaining Power of the Poor*. Bangladesh Development Studies, January-March 1978.

McNamara, Robert S. *One Hundred Countries, Two Billion People*. London: Praeger, 1973.

Meadows, Donella H. et al. *The Limits to Growth: A Report for the Club of Rome's Project on the Predicament of Mankind*. 2nd ed. New York: Universe Books, 1974.

Meier, Gerald M. *The International Economics of Development: Theory and Policy*. London: Harper & Row, 1968.

Meier, Gerald M. *Leading Issues in Development Economics*. London: Oxford University Press, 1970.

Mesarovic, Mihaljo and Pestel, Edward. *Mankind at the Turning Point: Second Report of the Club of Rome*. London: Hutchinson, 1975.

Minear, Larry. *New Hope for the Hungry?* New York: Friendship Press, 1975.

More Help for the Poorest: The Changing Emphasis in British Aid Policies. London: HMSO, Cmnd. 6270, reprinted 1977.

Morgan, Theodore. *Economic Development: Concept and Strategy*. New York: Harper, 1975.

Morton, Kathryn and Tulloch, Peter. *Trade and Developing Countries.* London: Croom Helm in association with ODI, 1977.

Mooneyham, W. Stanley. *What Do You Say to a Hungry World?* Waco, Texas: Word Books, 1975.

Myint, Hla. *The Economics of Developing Countries.* London: Hutchinson, 1965.

Myrdal, Gunnar. *The Challenge of World Poverty.* London: Penguin, 1970.

Myrdal, Gunnar. *Economic Theory and Underdeveloped Regions.* London: Duckworth, 1957.

Myrdal, Gunnar. *Asian Drama: an Inquiry into the Poverty of Nations.* London: Penguin, 1972.

Passell, Peter and Ross, Leonard. *The Retreat from Riches: Affluence and its Enemies.* New York: Viking, 1974.

Pearson, Lester B. et al. *Partners in Development: Report of the Commission on International Development.* London: Pall Mall, 1969.

Rich, William. *Smaller Families through Social and Economic Progress.* Washington: Overseas Development Council, 1973.

Schumacher, E. F. *Small is Beautiful: Economics as if People Mattered.* London: Sphere, 1974.

Seers, D. and Joy, L. *Development in a Divided World.* London: Penguin, 1971.

Simon, Arthur. *Bread for the World.* Grand Rapids and Paramus: Eerdmans and Paulist Press, 1975.

Singer, Hans and Ansari, Javid. *Rich and Poor Countries.* London: Allen & Unwin, 1977.

Singer, Hans. *Strategy of International Development.* London: Macmillan, 1975.

Stoesz, Edgar. *Beyond Good Intentions.* Akron, Pa.: Mennonite Central Committee, 1972.

Tinbergen, Jan, coordinator. *Reshaping the International Order: Report to the Club of Rome.* London: Hutchinson, 1977.

Towards a New International Economic Order. Report by Commonwealth Experts Group. London: Commonwealth Secretariat, 1977.

Unctad: A Fourth Choice. IDS Bulletin, Vol. 7, No 4.

Ward, Barbara. *A People Strategy of Development.* New York: Overseas Development Council, 1973.

World Bank. *Assault on World Poverty: Problems of Rural Development, Education and Health.* Baltimore: Johns Hopkins University Press, 1975.

REFERENCE WORKS

ABC of Development Assistance: Some International Terms and Institutions. Available from Information Dept., Ministry of Overseas Development, London.

British Aid Statistics, 1973-1977. ODM/HMSO.

Development Cooperation: Efforts and Policies of Member Countries of the Development Assistance Committee. Organization for Economic Cooperation and Development. Review published annually.

Sewell, John W. et al. *U.S. and World Development Agenda* 1977. London: Praeger, 1977, See also Howe, James W. (ed.). *The U.S. and World Development: Agenda for Action*, 1975.

Understanding Aid Stastistics. What is British Aid? Both available from Information Dept., Ministry of Overseas Development.

World Bank Annual Report.

Most of these books can be read at either the Ministry of Overseas Development (ODM), or the Overseas Development Institute (ODI).

LIFESTYLE

Ewald, Ellen Buchman. *Recipes for a Small Planet*. New York: Ballantine Books, 1973.

Gish, Arthur G. *Beyond the Rat Race*. Scottdale: Herald Press, 1973.

Lappe, Francis Moore. *Diet for a Small Planet*. Revised ed. New York: Ballantine, 1975.

Longacre, Doris Janzen. *More-with-Less Cookbook*. Lion, 1977.

Third Way. Enough is as Good as a Feast. January 1979.

THEOLOGY, BIBLICAL STUDIES AND THE CHURCH

Cosby, Gordon. *Handbook for Mission Groups*. Waco, Texas: Word Books, 1975.

Dayton, Donald W. *Discovering an Evangelical Heritage*. New York: Harper, 1976.

Gollwitzer, Helmut. *The Rich Christians and Poor Lazarus*. Trans. David Cairns. Edinburgh : St Andrews Press, 1970.

Harper, Michael. *A New Way of Living*. London: Hodder & Stoughton, 1974.

Hengel, Martin. *Property and Riches in the Early Church: Aspects of a Social History of Early Christianity*. Trans. John Bowden. London: SCM Press, 1974.

Kerans, Patrick. *Sinful Social Structures*. New York: Paulist Press, 1974.

Miranda, José. *Marx and the Bible: A Critique of the Philosophy of Oppression*. Trans. John Eagleson. London: SCM Press, 1977.

Morris, Colin. *Include Me Out! Confessions of an Ecclesiastical Coward*. London: Fontana, 1975.

Taylor, John V. *Enough is Enough*. London: SCM Press, 1975.

Wallis, James. *Agenda for Biblical People*. New York: Harper, 1976.

British Organizations

Amnesty International Amnesty International works for the relief of Prisoners of Conscience, and campaigns against torture, the death penalty, and other serious violations of human rights. A wide range of information available on request. 55 Theobalds Road, London WC1.

The Catholic Fund for Overseas Development (CAFOD) Official aid agency of the Catholic bishops of England and Wales. Speakers, posters, material and information can be provided. 21A Soho Square, London W1V 6NR.

Catholic Institute for International Relations (CIIR) Independent Catholic organization which promotes understanding within the United Kingdom on international relations, particularly overseas development. It publishes material suitable for use with adult groups, and produces a regular newsbrief, *Comment*, on issues of current international importance, and *CIIR News Quarterly*. 1 Cambridge Terrace, London NW1 4JL.

Centre for World Development Education (CWDE) Independent educational organization whose main aim is to increase knowledge and understanding in Britain of world development and the developing countries. CWDE publishes a wide range of written and visual materials. Parnell House, 25 Wilton Road, London SW1V 1JS.

Christian Aid Official development and relief agency of the British Council of Churches. It offers free and sale publications, posters, simulation games, filmstrips and films: catalogues free. P.O. Box No 1, London SW9 8BH.

Commonwealth Secretariat The Secretariat is responsible to and financed by the 36 independent nations of the Commonwealth, and is the main instrument of multilateral cooperation between them. It provides technical assistance, advisers, experts and training to Commonwealth developing countries. Free publications list, information office. Marlborough House, London SW1Y 5HX.

The Haslemere Group Independent voluntary organization founded in 1968 to discuss the social and economic crisis facing the developing countries. The Group welcomes postal enquiries and new members. c/o 467 Caledonian Road, London N7 9BE.

Help the Aged Help the Aged seeks to promote the welfare of the elderly in Britain and the Third World, both by fund raising and by public campaigning. Posters, wall charts, booklets and other publications, films and slides. Callers welcome. 32 Dover Street, London W1A 2AP.

The Institute of Development Studies (IDS) The Institute of Development Studies was set up by ODM in 1966 as a national centre concerned with Third World development and with the relationships between rich and poor countries. The library, which is open to individual researchers, contains publications from most Third World countries and is an official UN depository. The Annual Report and an IDS publications catalogue available. University of Sussex, Brighton BN1 9RE.

Intermediate Technology Development Group Ltd (ITDG) Non-profit organization concerned with the publication and dissemination of information on low-cost small-scale equipment and processes appropriate to the needs and resources of developing countries. A leaflet describing its work and a publications list from 9 King Street, Covent Garden, London WC2E 8HN.

Ministry of Overseas Development (ODM) ODM is responsible for the management of the British Government's aid programme to developing countries. Official reports and annual statistics are available from HMSO. A list of publications and other material, and a film catalogue, are available free, and the library is open on weekdays. Information Department, ODM, Eland House, Stag Place, London SW1E 5DH.

Overseas Development Institute (ODI) Independent research organization set up to provide a centre for research in development problems. Free publications list available. Library open on weekdays: inquiries and visitors welcome. 10–11 Percy Street, London W1P OJB.

Oxfam Independent voluntary organization campaigning to involve as many people as possible in the cause of world development and to raise funds for relief and development projects. Free and sale publications, posters and films. Catalogue. 274 Banbury Road, Oxford OX2 7DZ.

Returned Volunteer Action (RVA) Independent United Kingdom association of ex-overseas volunteers, together with those who support its aims. Access is offered through its clearing house to people who have worked in the Third World – for consultation, seminars and involvement with Third World and development issues; critical information on volunteering; and the distribution of some relevant publications. 1c Cambridge Terrace, Regent's Park, London NW1 4JI

The Save the Children Fund Independent voluntary organization concerned with the welfare of children throughout the world, particularly in the developing countries. Publications and posters about its organization, the health and education of children in developing countries and its work in disaster areas, slides and films. 157 Clapham Road, London SW9 OPT.

Third World First (3W1) Independent voluntary movement of students and other young people, encouraging action and understanding on the causes of poverty and underdevelopment. Publications include catalogues of Third World music and films available in the United Kingdom, posters, a fund-raising pack and an activists' handbook. Catalogue free, SAE if possible. 232 Cowley Road, Oxford OX4 1UH.

Third World Publications Ltd (TWP) TWP, a non-profit making company, distributes books from and about the Third World. It has stocks of development literature published both in Britain and overseas, as well as imports of African, Indian and Caribbean books, and books on theology. Free catalogue. 151 Stratford Road, Birmingham B11 1RD.

United Nations Children's Fund (UNICEF) UNICEF is financed entirely by voluntary contributions. It is now mainly concerned with long term development programmes meeting the basic needs of children. It has free and sale publications, posters, slide sets and films. Free catalogue. United Kingdom Committee for UNICEF, 46–8 Osnaburgh Street, London NW1 3PU.

United Nations Information Centre (UNIC) UNIC, a Secretariat office of the United Nations Headquarters in New York, provides materials on the work of the United Nations and its specialized agencies. Free publications available in limited quantities to teachers; sale publications may be purchased through HMSO. Reference library open on Mondays, Wednesdays and Thursdays. 14–15 Stratford Place, London W1N 9AF.

War on Want Independent voluntary organization to inform the British public about poverty, aid and development in the Third World. Free and sale publications, posters and films. Publications list. 467 Caledonian Road, London N7 9BE.

World Development Movement (WDM) Independent voluntary organization of local action groups concerned to campaign on the political issues of aid and development. Catalogue of free and sale publications. 26 Bedford Chambers Covent Garden, London WC2E 8HA.

The Shaftesbury Project The Shaftesbury Project is an initiative by evangelical Christians to consider the implications of involvement in society and to provide a biblical understanding of social and political action. As well as a study group working in the area of Overseas Aid and Development, the Project also has study groups engaged in political action, race relations, crime and punishment, the environment, work and leisure, the role of women, etc. It organizes conferences and seminars for Christians concerned for informed thinking and action in these fields, and also publishes booklets, papers, study guides, etc., to further these aims. Information can be obtained from The Director, The Shaftesbury Project, 8 Oxford Street, Nottingham NG1 5BH.

Tear Fund (The Evangelical Alliance Relief Fund) TEAR Fund is an interdenominational evangelical relief and development agency working through missionaries and national Christian leaders. In addition to the support of projects and personnel overseas, it runs a child-sponsorship programme. Educational literature for all ages is published, together with audio-visual aids and publicity material. Free catalogue from 11 Station Road, Teddington, Middlesex. TW11 9AA

Christian Aid Christian Aid is the official development and relief agency of the British Council of Churches. In addition to its funding of projects in the developing countries, it maintains an extensive educational programme in Britain, both through a specialist London-based staff and through a team of area secretaries, to explore the relationship between development and underdevelopment. It has free and sale publications, posters, simulation games, filmstrips and films, most of which are intended for educational use. Catalogues of both publications and audio-visual aids are available free on request. P.O Box No 1, London SW9 8BH

Tearcraft Tearcraft is a Christian organization importing handicrafts and cottage industry products from the Third World producers. They are sold through a mail order catalogue, and by selling direct to shops, other groups and societies at wholesale rates. Further information and a free catalogue, Carliol Square, Newcastle upon Tyne NE1 6UF.

Biblical References

223